Japanese Maverick

Japanese Maverick

Success Secrets of Canon's "God of Sales"

Louis Kraar

Seiichi Takikawa

JOHN WILEY & SONS, INC.

New York • Chichester • Brisbane • Toronto • Singapore

Library of Congress Cataloging-in-Publication Data:

Kraar, Louis, 1931–
  Japanese maverick : success secrets of Canon's "god of sales" /
Louis Kraar and Seiichi Takikawa.
    p. cm.
  ISBN 0-471-58011-2 (acid-free paper)
  1. Sales management—Japan—Case studies. 2. Kyanon Hanbai
Kabushiki Kaisha.—Management—Case studies. 3. Takikawa, Seiichi,
1931–   .—Career in sales management. 4. Success in business—
Japan—Case studies. I. Takikawa, Seiichi, 1931–   . II. Title.
HF5438.4.K73 1993
658.8'1'00952—dc20   93-8808
Printed in the United States of America

10 9 8 7 6 5 4 3 2 1

Printed and bound by Courier Companies, Inc.

Acknowledgments

A book, like life itself, benefits from teachers, friends, and valued colleagues too numerous to list in a single volume. We owe a special debt to many who assisted in our research and preparation.

Among those in the Canon Group who actively participated in this work (in alphabetical order) are: Takashi Fujimura, Hirosuke Fujiwara, Masaya Fukushima, Hajime Hirai, Hideo Irimajiri, Hiroto Kagami, Tohru Kaneko, Hiroshi Kobayashi, Hitoshi Kohnomori, Takashi Kuroe, Tomomasa Matsui, Hideharu Takemoto, Mitsuru Tamai, Yoshiyuki Todaka, Hedeo Tani, and Keizo Yamaji.

Others who contributed their insights and time include (again in alphabetical order): Takashi Inoue, president of Inoue Public Relations Inc.; Nobuo Kanai, chairman of Micro Systems Sales Co. Ltd.; Kazuyoshi Kino, president of the Hosen Women's College; Diane Nakamura of the Rowland Company in New York; Masami Nakamura, president of Chiba Sokki Co., Ltd.; Akira Nishigaki, president and chairman of the board of the Overseas Economic Corporation Fund; Shuji Takashina, director general of the National Museum of Western Art in Tokyo; Vittorio Volpi, senior representative in Japan for Banca della Svizzera Italiana (the Swiss-Italian Bank).

We are grateful to all of these people, as well as many others not mentioned here.

Contents

CONTENTS

Introduction

his is the tale of Seiichi Takikawa, an extraordinary executive who is setting a new tone for Japan. He eagerly sells American products in Japan, insists that employees refresh themselves by taking long vacations, and prods fellow Japanese to become more cosmopolitan. A rarity in Japan, Takikawa is an outspoken entrepreneur within a large organization, Canon Inc. This Japanese group of companies is exceptional in having a highly flexible and creative corporate culture, which encourages upstarts like Takikawa.

Canon, which started as a tiny lab making a clone of the German Leica camera, has blossomed into one of the world's top makers of copiers, a leading producer of office equipment, and a technological innovator. Much of Canon's patented know-how winds up in American products. Canon Inc. is not only a major manufacturer of precision machines that etch computer chips, but it also supplies the engines for most laser printers. In 1992, Canon obtained 1,106 U.S. patents—more than such well-known companies as General Electric, IBM, Eastman Kodak, and Motorola. With worldwide sales of more than $15 billion annually, Canon ranked eighty-third in size (bigger than Lockheed and Coca-Cola) on the 1992 *Fortune* Global 500 list of industrial corporations. Genuinely global, Canon has 26 manufacturing plants scattered around the world from California to China, plus research facilities in the United States, Europe, and Australia.

To American eyes, the Japanese people often look like devoted drones of an economic superpower that relentlessly exports its own goods but protects its home market from foreign goods. Indeed, hardworking Japanese subordinate their individuality to the greater good of their companies, putting in longer hours for less pay than their counterparts in Western countries. Only about half of Japanese employ-

3

ees take their *full* paid vacation (an average of only twelve days a year, about half the vacation time of Americans). The Japanese sacrifice free time partly out of fear of letting down the team. Above all, they cherish a sense of belonging. The South Koreans, who have long put in even more hours than the Japanese, have been quicker to figure out that leisure is one of the rewards of economic prosperity. As Ungsuh K. Park, president of Samsung Petrochemical Co. in Korea, puts it, "All Japanese live under the terror of being different. Conformity is of cardinal importance to the Japanese, while we Koreans are a bunch of cowboys."

The immediate rewards for shareholders of Japanese corporations are meager, too. Dividends amount to about 30 percent of profits, about half the level paid out by American companies. Most Japanese corporate earnings are reinvested in new equipment, factories, or cash reserves for stormy times. This long-term strategy is made possible by a unique brand of capitalism. Some 70 percent of the stock in Japanese companies is owned by other corporations, usually members of groups called *keiretsu*, which are linked by cross-share holdings and long-term business relationships. Under this clubby arrangement, companies usually prefer doing business with members of their own group—an inherent trade barrier.

Canon, which belongs to no *keiretsu*, is more open and independent than most other Japanese companies. The Fuji Bank, though loosely associated with Canon, has no representatives on its board and no great influence on Canon's operations. In contrast, the Japanese camera maker Nikon is effectively part of the huge Mitsubishi Group. Nikon has not diversified as widely as Canon, apparently to avoid competition with other Mitsubishi companies. Remarks a senior Canon executive, "Every unit in Canon can freely do what it wants, provided that the funds can be raised."

Japanese corporate chief executives (even at Canon) tirelessly devote themselves to companies—for relatively modest pay. Presidents of large Japanese companies earn about one-third of what their U.S. counterparts make: The Japanese chief executives average about $375,000 a year, compared with $1.2 million paid to top American executives, according to a survey by the Wage and Salary Administration Research Institute in Japan. The Japanese, of course, enjoy other forms of compensation, not only generous expense accounts and company cars, but also enormous prestige among subordinates. As one Japanese senior executive confides, "I'm treated almost like a god."

Canon, however, has long anticipated a new attitude that is gradually taking shape in Japan: There's more to life than incessantly flooding the world with more and more goods made in Japan. Canon, in fact, has decided that its ultimate survival depends on providing its Japanese employees with more leisure and on spreading its manufacturing and research operations (as well as their profits) to other countries.

Lately, other Japanese business leaders have begun seriously questioning the results of a system that has created a rich country with a surprisingly poor quality of life. A new word has taken root in Japan: *karoshi*, death from overwork. In the past few years, the Labor Ministry has awarded compensation to some 30 families whose breadwinners died under the pressures of overwork. Akio Morita, the respected chairman of Sony and a challenger of conventional wisdom, has urged Japanese corporations to change their ways of competing because the tolerance of Western rivals "is reaching its limit." Among other things, Morita wants Japanese companies to give employees more free time and higher salaries. Corporations in Japan, he says, should stress profits ahead of constantly expanding market shares and should give stockholders bigger dividends.

Likewise, the Japanese government, which tends to be deferential to the interests of big business, has proclaimed a new goal: The decade of the 1990s is supposed to transform the workaholic nation into a "life-style superpower" where Japanese can finally enjoy life. Setting an example, the government has ordered its 1.1 million employees to observe a five-day work week in a country where most employees still show up at offices and factories on Saturdays. Nonetheless, many Japanese put in long hours of overtime for which they hardly ever claim payment.

Fundamental changes in Japan will take time but cannot be delayed much longer. The high costs of manufacturing many standard products in Japan, from air conditioners to television sets, have forced Japanese companies to relocate factories to other Asian countries. The supply of labor in Japan itself is tight; the work force is aging. The graying of Japan, which has the highest average life expectancy in the world, will have profound effects. By the year 2020, more than 20 percent of Japanese will be over 65 years old, imposing huge costs in pensions, medical care, and other social-welfare programs. And, already, younger Japanese want more pleasure in life than the joy of simply being a good company man or woman.

Takikawa, who grew up with Canon, provides an inside view of life at a leading Japanese corporation, plus instructive techniques for being a leader, motivating employees, and promoting sales. His lessons on business are gleaned from experiences of an unconventional career: Takikawa has worked as a messenger, a hotel room boy, a labor union leader, a director of personnel, and a pioneer for Canon products in the U.S. market. Now chairman and chief executive of Canon Sales Co., an independent marketing arm in Japan, Takikawa has transformed what he describes as a formerly "sleeping company" into a powerhouse for selling both Canon products and American computers in Japan. As he puts it, "Rather than being a figurehead in Canon Inc., I'm the experimenter in major corporate strategic approaches."

His and Canon's story unfolds in two dimensions in this book. In Part One, this writer looks inside the Japanese organization to reveal the roots of its success, its future thrust, and the rise of the maverick Takikawa. In Part Two, Takikawa shares his distinctive approaches to building business. Unusual as he is in Japan, Takikawa purveys management ideas that are applicable almost anywhere.

Part One

Inside Canon, a Haven for Creativity and Upstarts

1

A Different Breed of Japanese

The nail that sticks up will be hammered down.

— an old Japanese
saying

Japan, for all its economic success, is a land of conformists. Its business leaders, usually colorless old men, profess to lead by politely deferring to the consensus of subordinates and sharing responsibility. The system provides everyone with a strong sense of security but makes individual Japanese amazingly adverse to taking risks. One notable exception is Seiichi Takikawa, 62, a Japanese maverick who constantly stirs up Canon Inc., the world's largest producer of cameras and copying machines. Bluntly outspoken, highly entrepreneurial, and swiftly decisive, Takikawa insists that selling "is a science" and eagerly supplies American products to his Japanese customers. Even admiring colleagues say that Takikawa manages "like a tyrant," aggressively pushing subordinates to carry out *his* ideas.

Glimpses of his youth show how this shiny nail escaped being hammered down:

In the aftermath of World War II, when Tokyo lay in rubble, Takikawa was a hungry teenager. He got vital schooling in the streets. Takikawa found part-time work at a small enterprise that refilled old shoe polish containers and peddled them on the black market. Hearing other employees, mostly housewives, complain of their low pay, Takikawa took up their cause with the proprietor—who instantly fired him. "I was fired from other jobs, too, simply because I was so self-righteous," he recalls. "After a while, I decided never to leave an employer in a way that I could not meet that guy again." Though he never completely muted his outspoken ways, he mastered the art of differing, even clashing, with people and yet not creating enemies.

Working nights as a room boy (a combination of butler and messenger) at the Ambassador Hotel while attending the elite University of Tokyo, Takikawa picked up another enduring lesson about human dignity. Some guests summoned him by shouting "Boy!"; but he always ran first to those who addressed him (more respectfully) as "boy-san." Says Takikawa, "I learned never to discriminate against anybody for any reason. If you deal with people fairly, they will trust and support you. And you can see it in their eyes."

LEARNING TO TAKE RISKS

Elected leader of Canon's union at the age of 30, Takikawa faced turmoil that made him dread waking up in the mornings. Communist activists sought to organize a rival union for temporary production workers, who earned less than regular employees. Takikawa made a bold gamble to squeeze out the radical activists: He offered those workers equal status with others, and then sold the idea to Canon's management.

"I'm a slightly different breed from most Japanese," admits Takikawa, "because I have taken a lot of risks." Climbing out on a limb as a labor union leader could have doomed his career. As it turned out, his skill at restoring harmony opened the way for Takikawa to prove himself in other tough assignments at Canon—including director of personnel—without having his unconventional methods questioned.

Five managers in succession failed to make significant inroads in the American market, but, in 1970, Takikawa took over and led a revolution. Overturning the long-established practice of relying on American companies to market Canon's products, Takikawa created his own sales force. He quickly made Canon U.S.A. a major supplier of cameras and office equipment. Hideharu Takemoto, who later served as president of Canon U.S.A., says of his predecessor, "Takikawa is a great thinker in marketing, but not an ordinary Japanese manager. He's always challenging things like an entrepreneurial American executive. He never gives up, even if it means fighting."

A NEW MARKETING APPROACH

Bucking tradition again, Takikawa returned to Tokyo in 1977 and woke up the dormant Canon Sales Co. by bringing U.S. computers and more aggressive salesmanship into the Japanese market. In Japan most salespeople are male. Takikawa assigns every new employee, including senior managers, to do a stint in retail sales. Top salesmen are rewarded with lavish ceremonial dinners, including one at a Tokyo restaurant that he describes as "reputed to offer the balls of a tiger." His company (with annual revenues of more than $4 billion) has the greatest "sales vitality" in Japan, according to a recent survey by the Japanese business publication *Nikkei Sangyo Shimbun*. Among other things, Takikawa has expanded Canon's market share for copiers from a mere 10 percent to 30 percent, the dominant position in Japan. Operating with much independence from Canon Inc., the parent company, he has even attained a separate listing on the Tokyo Stock Exchange for Canon Sales Co.

Above all, Takikawa senses that Japan requires a new approach to marketing. He believes that the country has entered a crucial third wave in its postwar business development. In the first two decades after World War II, Japanese companies could sell almost anything they turned out and, thus, left marketing to outside distributors. Then, starting in the mid-1960s, Japan entered what Takikawa terms "the era of excess supply," the second wave, which forced Canon and other manufacturers into *pushing* their products onto both retailers and consumers rather than waiting for the products to be bought. The latest and third wave, which began when Japan encountered sharp trade frictions with the United States and Europe in the mid-1980s, is *two-way global marketing*. Canon, for instance, not only makes its copiers in the United States, Germany, and France, but increasingly relies on selling other imported products to satisfy its Japanese customers.

In this new era, says Takikawa, "real sales activity begins *after* you sell." In other words, salespeople must become expert consultants to their customers. Often the easiest way to sell a Canon laser printer in Japan, for example, is by offering it along with an Apple Macintosh computer and American software. Takikawa's theory: Loyal users of Canon copiers and printers will buy packages of sophisticated, interconnected computer equipment if Canon Sales Co. can assemble the system and make it easy to use. Betting over $200 million on this strategy, Takikawa is building a new software development center to link Canon's optical and image capabilities with computers—which gives him more to sell. So far, he offers over 150 software products to link Canon color copiers with computers.

This is a potentially powerful strategy because Canon Sales is already the world's leading Apple Macintosh computer dealer and a significant purveyor of IBM personal computers. The recent price war among personal computers has spread to Japan, spurring sales of many brands and creating a great opportunity for Canon. Says Takikawa,

"The reason this reinforces demand for our products is simple. Every personal computer sold will require peripheral equipment, such as printers. Canon controls more than 70 percent of the worldwide market for laser printers and is a top supplier of Bubble-Jet printers."

CHRISTIANITY, BUDDHISM, AND EINSTEIN

While putting faith in high technology, Takikawa also earnestly believes that marketing is his God-given mission. He sums it up with his own motto: "Appreciating fully one's calling, living and acting with freedom." Explains Takikawa, "Everyone's career is really determined by God, who gave us the ability to recognize opportunities and create things. Using that talent fully is fulfilling our obligations to an omnipotent being." Having made a hobby of studying theology, he sees little distinction among religions: "I believe in essence that Christianity, Buddhism, and the philosophy of Einstein are all the same. Each religion is mainly a point of entry in climbing a tall mountain."

In the bland Japanese business world, Takikawa attracts attention and loyal followers. Vittorio Volpi, the senior representative in Tokyo for the Swiss-Italian Bank (Banca della Svizzera Italiana), has lived in the country for two decades, speaks Japanese, knows dozens of Japanese chief executives, and says, "Definitely, Takikawa is the one who has impressed me the most." Takikawa is not only open and decisive in business, adds Volpi, but is among the very few Japanese executives who enjoy discussing literature, philosophy, and religion. Takikawa talks comfortably about historical novels or Buddhist theology, but never seems to be showing off his considerable knowledge. Remarks the European banker, "This society does not like strong leaders, but he survives by knowing how to play the game."

Takikawa works hard at sounding modest, for instance. He makes self-deprecating jokes about frequenting bars and performing erratically as a student. Says Takikawa, "That's why, even today, my friends include both bright members of the elite as well as people who are really hopeless cases." In fact, he is an intellectual with a common touch. His rugged youth in the streets of Tokyo attuned Takikawa to the feelings of manual laborers, shopkeepers, and messengers—the sort of people few members of the Japanese business elite know. He has a gift for establishing rapport with just about anybody.

A WET AND DRY PERSONALITY

Besides constantly tossing out new marketing ideas, Takikawa knows how to make them exciting to the Japanese dealers who sell Canon products. These operators of relatively small businesses, Canon's primary customers, are generally cautious about everything except Takikawa. "I've never met anyone like him in 30 years of business life—and probably never will again," says Nobuo Kanai, chairman of Micro Systems Sales Co., Ltd., a longtime distributor of Canon office products. He hastens to add that, as a customer, he has no motive for "apple-polishing," but really sees a highly unusual man. Explains Kanai: "Takikawa embodies two opposing elements—the very dry approach of Western-style business that seeks efficiency and economy, plus the wet Oriental personality that cares about human relationships."

That "wet" quality, the ability to project an overwhelming empathy with others, is crucial to Japanese dealers. As Kanai puts it, "Having a drink with Takikawa makes you feel very comfortable. He's completely open and can really read another person's feelings. You can take off your kimono, so to speak, and discuss anything without getting hurt or embarrassed." Another dealer, who describes Takikawa as "a god of sales," admits to having been skeptical that Canon could become the number one supplier of copiers when it started as a relatively minor player. Takikawa told him that if you believe in something long enough, it will happen. Persuading the dealers to believe in him, of course, made all the difference.

Within Canon, Takikawa usually gets to do things his way by forceful use of facts, logic, and a persistence that bulldozes opposition. Remarks Takashi Fujimura, a managing director at Canon Sales, "I have been under his control for about 20 years. He's very tough. I respect him and try to meet his requests, but I almost die doing it. He listens to other managers, of course, but decides everything." Takikawa's approach would never raise an eyebrow in an American executive suite, but, in the Japanese business world of consensus management, he seems almost like a giant who roars.

Takikawa's ability to survive—and prosper—in a large Japanese corporation tells a lot about Canon. The company is almost as unconventional as Takikawa.

2

Canon's "Doctor" Was Always on Duty

Japan is a small country without natural resources.
The only things we can depend on are the brains and
diligence of the Japanese people.

—Dr. Takeshi Mitarai, the late founder of Canon

physician with limited business experience, Dr.
Takeshi Mitarai led Canon's dazzling postwar growth
almost by accident. He bankrolled Precision Optical
Research Laboratory, established in 1933, to develop Japan's
first 35 mm camera with a focal-plane shutter. That lab
sprouted into Canon. Eventually drawn into the business,
Dr. Mitarai nurtured the venture into a global corporation by
relying on young managers.

Originally a passive investor, Dr. Mitarai concentrated
on treating patients and delivering babies at the obstetrics
department of the Japanese Red Cross Hospital in Tokyo
and then established his own practice. When no one else
was available to run the fledgling company during World
War II, Dr. Mitarai reluctantly stepped in. After the war, he
stayed on because rebuilding Japanese industry seemed
more exciting to him than returning to his medical practice.
Under Dr. Mitarai, Canon Camera Co., as it was renamed in
1947, expanded into microfilm equipment, electronic calculators, office equipment, and much more—emerging as a
technology leader in the information industry with its present
name *Canon Inc.*

Dr. Mitarai shaped Canon largely as a father figure,
delegating most decisions to hand-picked subordinates.
Even the customs and rituals of Japanese business were
somewhat alien to him. As a physician, he was accustomed
to having everyone bow to him respectfully and defer to his

judgment. Remarks a Canon executive, "It was very difficult to take Dr. Mitarai into a bank because he would not bow in deference to bankers." Nonetheless, he had a great talent for judging character and thrusting responsibility on men in their thirties—remarkable in a society that almost worships seniority. Dr. Mitarai's postwar protégés now run Canon. Ryuzaburo Kaku, who at the age 36 was put in charge of the company's finances and administration, is now chairman of Canon Inc. Keizo Yamaji, who supervised technology for Dr. Mitarai, is now vice-chairman of Canon Inc.

Takikawa, now the master of marketing at Canon Sales Co. and another of the physician's bright young men, says, "It was really simple to work for Dr. Mitarai. After all, he was an M.D. and didn't know the details of business practices. He would leave them to you. When you are trusted so much, you just have to do a job well."

BRUSHING ASIDE SENIORITY

Besides being relatively innocent about how things were customarily done in Japanese corporations, Dr. Mitarai believed that creating a meritocracy was sensible. He once remarked, "In Japan, seniority is often regarded as the main factor in selecting executives. But unless a man's capability is good, I don't put him in a position. I don't care if he is not even a college graduate as long as the person has ability." Consequently, Dr. Mitarai appointed Takikawa, then only 39, as president of Canon U.S.A. And in 1977 the founder made Kaku, who then ranked fifth in seniority, president of Canon Inc.

The doctor's unconventional approach to management (at least in Japan) made Canon a haven for experimentation and creativity. In its early days, Canon more closely resembled an American venture firm than a tightly organized Japanese corporation. Recalls Dr. Yamaji, "We were able to conduct research and any other kind of work in a very free atmosphere. And a failure was not counted against a young person if there were good intentions behind it. You could recover by an achievement later." That attitude of exceptional freedom became the essence of an enduring corporate culture.

When this writer met the late Dr. Mitarai in 1980, Canon's founder, at the age of 79, was still company chairman and adviser to the young executives he had installed. Dr. Mitarai described his role as "looking down at the company from the mountain top." He looked and acted like a wise grandfather—with patches of gray hair on the side of his head, his skin as fine as old parchment, his eyes alert. Dr. Mitarai took special pleasure in showing up first at Canon's headquarters every working day. As he explained it, "I like to study the faces of executives as they arrive and perform a visual physical exam to see if they are healthy."

AN AWARD FOR HAPPY FAMILY LIFE

Highly moralistic, Dr. Mitarai created for Canon employees a slogan called GHQ (Go Home Quickly). He was campaigning against Japanese men regularly stopping off to drink with colleagues after work, still a custom in the country. Discussing his GHQ drive at our meeting in 1980, Dr. Mitarai said, "I was very popular among the wives, though not so much among all the husbands." Taking the campaign even further, he also handed out a special award to every employee who had a peaceful family life. How could he judge that? After much thought, Dr. Mitarai decided that the best way to gauge the tranquility of a worker's home was by his attendance record. He told me: "If a husband drops by a bar after work instead of going home, there will be a quarrel with his wife in the morning—and he'll be late to work."

Dr. Mitarai wound up leading Canon because a close friend persuaded him to support its predecessor, the tiny optical lab. The scientific challenge appealed to the doctor, who told this writer, "At that time, it was only seven or eight years after my graduation from medical school, where even the microscopes that we used were made in Germany. So I thought this kind of business was right for Japan." He also liked the people who had set up the research venture in a Tokyo apartment. "It was a kind of comrade-like relationship," he remarked. "To register a company, you needed seven organizers, and we were all good friends."

Precision Optical Research Laboratory was the idea of Goro Yoshida, who spent his boyhood taking cameras apart to see how they were made and started producing movie projectors in the late 1920s. He enlisted Saburo Uchida, his brother-in-law and a stockbroker, as a partner in the lab. In turn, Uchida approached Dr. Mitarai for financial aid to start the business. The lab made a prototype of Japan's first 35 mm camera called Kwanon (the origin of the company's present name) and, in 1934, teamed up to get its lens manufactured for another model with Nikon—now a Canon rival.

When Uchida got drafted into the army early in World War II, Dr. Mitarai divided his time between overseeing the optical lab and treating patients at his hospital. "I felt both were helping the country," said Dr. Mitarai. Under his influence, in 1940, the fledgling company made Japan's first indirect X-ray camera, which played a major role in eradicating tuberculosis in the country.

THE TRAGEDY OF MADE-IN-JAPAN

The foresight of Dr. Mitarai propelled the postwar rise of Canon. During the U.S. occupation of Japan in 1950, he visited America for the first time to study the market and discovered firsthand that a "Made-in-Japan" label meant cheap and shabby products. As Dr. Mitarai put it, "Japan made things sold only in 10-cent stores." Once home, he vividly described the nation's problem in a magazine article entitled "The Tragedy of Made-in-Japan." Dr. Mitarai decided that unless Japan could produce quality products at reasonable prices, as he put it, "we could not do business in America." Instead of theorizing about the problem, he set about reeducating Canon's workers, who ultimately turned out world-class cameras. In 1960, Canon introduced its first popular 35 mm compact camera, the Canonet, which was equipped with an "electronic eye" that freed the user from having to set the lens opening.

Other innovative products followed, enabling Canon to keep reinventing itself. The camera company, for instance, quickly diversified into office equipment, now the bulk of its business. In 1964, Canon introduced the first 10-key electronic calculator (the kind everyone uses today), which replaced models with the large keyboard like those on old-fashioned cash registers. That pioneering ten-key model, called Canola 130, took up as much space as one of today's desktop computers. Canon, however, neglected to patent its keyboard arrangement, which was adopted by every other maker of calculators.

Canon invented new kinds of copying machines, though they were little noticed initially. Spurred in the early 1960s by an Arthur D. Little study that *minimized* chances of a breakthrough that could threaten Xerox's dominance of the copier business, Canon developed a challenge to the American company. Canon's New Process, NP for short, was the first plain-paper alternative to Xerography. The NP copier drum had an insulating layer that permitted using a more photosensitive chemical than Xerox machines of those days. More importantly, the NP copier made Canon completely free of relying on Xerox patents. But the company lacked the sales organization to do much immediately with its edge.

Canon blew another breakthrough in 1972, when its designers patented a technique for further simplifying copying machines and slashing their costs. The "liquid-dry" system—so named because it uses liquid developer and turns out dry copies on plain paper—ended up being licensed to 20 Japanese manufacturers and three in the United States. In 1980, about half the plain–paper copiers in use incorporated some of Canon's technology, but few consumers knew it. Spreading the know-how around so quickly, a senior Canon executive later admitted, was "a bad decision." The company acted out of fear that competitors would infringe on its patents anyway and from lack of confidence in Canon's own marketing power.

LEARNING TO STORM WORLD MARKETS

Profiting from its past errors, Canon stormed world markets in 1979 with a new typewriter-size copier called NP-200. Its compactness resulted from more technical innovations, including a single-component dry developer (not immediately licensed to rivals) and fiber optics that replaced bulky lenses and mirrors. Gradually, Canon learned how to translate its creations into commercial successes. By the 1980s, its small copiers and laser printers (another Canon invention) were equipped with replaceable cartridges containing everything that could run out or wear out—making them virtually maintenance free.

Always clever at inventing things, Canon finally took off by strengthening its marketing. Takikawa provided much of that sales power in both America and later Japan, underpinned by a new way of developing products at Canon: The company's initial designers, in effect, are marketing specialists. One dramatic result is the AE-1 camera, which Canon introduced in 1976 as the "world's first" computer-controlled single lens reflex (SLR) camera. It made professional-quality 35 mm photography readily accessible to amateurs and became the world's best-selling SLR camera.

The AE-1 camera started not with a gleam in an inventor's eye, but through concern in the company about the sluggish growth of SLR photography. That field was mainly for specialists who could pay $500 or more for a camera and did not mind constantly fiddling with its controls. Masahiro Tanaka, a company planner who studied the market back then, says, "We figured that if this intellectual's camera were made simple to use and 20 percent less expensive, we could surely sell more." To produce a high-tech camera at a fairly low price, Canon had to devise new manufacturing methods—such as using metal-coated plastic for parts of the body. The biggest gamble was investing heavily in mass-production equipment in hopes that the camera would be a hit among consumers.

To improve the odds of success, Canon plotted its sales campaign even before the camera was developed. Canon U.S.A. contributed $150,000 to the 1976 Summer Olympics in Montreal, and the AE-1 became the "official camera" of many top sports events of the day. Takikawa boldly invested in national network television commercials, the first ever used to promote a Japanese camera in America.

As a result, Canon created what one industry analyst described as "the Chevrolet of the 35 mm camera market."

A HAPPY ACCIDENT IN THE LAB

Ever since then, Canon has not only continued pouring out original products, but also made customers notice them. Most dramatically, Canon machines turn out color copies that are difficult to distinguish from the original. Canon also developed Bubble-Jet technology for computer printers, literally spraying tiny drops of ink on paper to create print as clear as a book. The Bubble-Jet principle was discovered in one of Canon's labs when a researcher accidentally brushed his soldering iron against the tip of an ink-filled syringe—and ink shot out of the needle. It took considerably more work, of course, to develop densely-packed microscopic nozzles to control the ink flow.

Canon's optical expertise has opened many other profitable doors. With the start of the TV age in the 1950s, Canon used its know-how originally developed for still cameras to make zoom lens for TV cameras. Now its video lenses are used widely for everything from showing viewers the Olympics to showing earthlings the universe as seen from the U.S. space shuttle *Columbia*. The computer chip, or integrated circuit, used in products ranging from autos to Walkman-type tape players, created another fine arena for Canon. The company makes specialized equipment to facilitate mass production of those chips. Making them entails transfering circuit patterns onto silicon wafers by a process known as *photolithography*, which borrows heavily from the photographic technology that Canon knows so well.

Having transformed itself into a technology leader, Canon is now spreading its research and development into other countries. The company has labs in the United States, Europe, and Australia. (Its American research centers specialize in developing computer hardware and software.) But Canon goes far beyond just tapping foreign brains and then manufacturing their creations in Japan; instead, a product designed in another country is made there. Canon Research Centre Europe Limited in Britain, for example, devised a new kind of stereo speaker system that uses optical principles; the product is now produced in the United Kingdom and sold throughout the world.

NOW COMES THE *KYOSEI* STRATEGY

Internationalizing both research and manufacturing is part of a Canon policy called *kyosei*, translated as "living and working together for the common good." Chairman Kaku readily acknowledges that many companies claim to operate under similar lofty principles, but insists that Canon actually implements *kyosei* as a strategic plan for everything it does. As a matter of basic principle, Canon also does *not* do certain things that could be profitable, including military research. The company will not make disposable cameras because Canon, Inc. says that "they are not environmentally sound." Its corporate plan focuses on "creating previously unexplored technologies and product categories" rather than being a copycat.

Besides bolstering Canon's image, *kyosei* is enlightened self-interest: Over 70 percent of Canon's sales are exports, which means that trade restrictions would be a disaster for the corporation. Many countries—especially the United States—have chronic trade deficits with Japan, so manufacturing products where they are sold helps Canon ease trading frictions. Moreover, ever-rising costs in Japan make it more economical to produce many of Canon's products in other countries.

No longer exclusively Japanese, Canon makes many of its cameras in such places as Taiwan, Malaysia, and China. Its office equipment and components are assembled in both the United States and Europe. A plant in Mexico puts together printed circuit boards for Canon products. Rather than trying to do everything itself, Canon forges alliances with American companies—including Eastman Kodak in the microfilm field. Likewise, Canon makes printers for Apple and sells Apple computers in Japan.

In 1990, Canon moved not only the entire production of its electronic typewriters to the United States, but everything to do with that business—including its headquarters and development work. Canon Business Machines in Costa Mesa, California, backed by Canon de Mexico, is a fully integrated manufacturing facility for electronic typewriters, desktop publishing systems, and fax machines. Giving up what had been a Japanese export makes a lot of business sense for Canon. Some 95 percent of the electronic typewriters are sold in North America and Europe, where typewriter exports have been the target of dumping charges. Dumping, that is, exporting a product at a price deemed to be below fair market value, can result in high punitive tariffs that effectively halt sales in a country.

PRESERVING HARMONY IN INTERNATIONAL TRADE

Canon responded to the dumping allegations by rethinking its typewriter business. Says Vice Chairman Yamaji, "Upon reflecting on why typewriters were the initial target [for dumping charges], I realized the West had been driven by necessity to invent the typewriter, which has since been used to set forth nearly all aspects of Western culture and civilization." He adds, "I became aware of our conceit with technology to produce typewriters in Japan and export most of them merely because Japan was somehow advanced in technology." Cynics might well conclude that the popularity of typewriters is fading anyway in this computer age, but Canon has also shifted to America its manufacturing of a new generation of products, such as desktop publishing systems.

To preserve trade harmony in Europe, Canon completely got out of making dot-matrix printers for computers. The problem erupted in 1988 when the European Community imposed antidumping duties on Japanese dot-matrix printers. To avoid paying the high tariffs, Japanese manufacturers suddenly built 12 printer plants in Europe. "I thought this was total insanity," says Dr. Yamaji. At the time, there were only a few European makers of such printers, and Canon feared that the Japanese would be perceived as destroying local industry. Bowing out of a product that was already mature, Canon specialized in more advanced Bubble-Jet printers that embody its own technology.

Having created copiers with disposable cartridges, Canon has mounted an ambitious global recycling program. Customers are encouraged to send in their used cartridges, which in the United States and Canada come with self-addressed envelopes. Canon ships those used cartridges to its plant in Dalian, China, where they are taken apart and recycled. The plastic casing, for example, is ground into particles, combined with some new plastic and binding material, and remolded for use as the outer casing of new cartridges. Recycling is no bargain for Canon, which calls its program the "Clean Earth Campaign," but the extra expense has yielded other returns: praise from environmentalists and an award in 1991 from the National Geographic Society. Canon hopes to extend its recycling to entire copier machines.

Since the days of Dr. Mitarai, Canon's technology and marketing have gone through immense changes, but not the company's basic character. It remains a creative up-start, unusually independent from the clubby groups that dominate Japanese business. After all, Canon is still run by the disciples of the physician who happened to become its leader. And none of them is a more rugged individualist than Seiichi Takikawa, the master of marketing.

3

The Making of a Maverick

I've probably argued and complained against the management more than anyone else in Canon. Yet I never made enemies. I've probably busted up more things and built my own things to replace them more than anyone else at Canon. But I learned never to destroy your last bridge.

—Seiichi Takikawa

$\mathcal{H}$ is incessant drive for change, says Takikawa, comes from growing up amid hardship. "Our generation has always been the marking point for change," says Takikawa. "We're not at all surprised, let alone shocked, by big changes in values. Almost overnight, we dropped to being the people of a defeated country." The first three postwar years were the hungriest time for Takikawa and his contemporaries. A high school classmate, Akira Nishigaki, who is now president and chairman of Japan's Overseas Economic Cooperation Fund, recalls, "Everyone suffered. Most basic food staples were rationed. As boys, everything put before us we ate. Those difficulties probably gave us more ambition."

War affected Takikawa early in his life. His father Mataji, an army officer in prewar Japan, was rarely at home. When Takikawa was only five years old, his parents divorced. Army tradition required Mataji to resign. In 1937, after remarrying, his father was drafted back into the military for the Sino-Japanese War—and did not return until the end of World War II. "My father kept going off to war," he now says, "so I don't have many memories of him."

As a boy of five, Takikawa boarded with other families for awhile, finally winding up with his stepmother Tomi. "She was a fantastic woman and really took care of me," he recalls. Just before the war ended, Takikawa's junior high

37

school class in Tokyo was mobilized to work in the Central Post Office. Air raids destroyed his house, so Takikawa fled with his stepmother to her home in Fukushima, then a rural town, in the middle of the main Japanese island of Honshu. There, he was ordered out of school again to work in a plant making aircraft parts. He says, half-jokingly, "The war is among my many excuses for not studying much."

Takikawa, in fact, was cramming like mad to pass the entrance exam for First High School in Tokyo, the path into the University of Tokyo, the nation's top institute of higher learning. He studied until 3 or 4 every morning. As Takikawa remembers it, "My stepmother always would bring me a snack at 1 A.M. She never missed a day. People from Fukushima are said to be very traditional parents, the kind you just don't find any more." Still, he flunked the exam and had to cram for another year until finally passing it.

PICKING UP THE PIECES AFTER WORLD WAR II

Standing outside Fukushima Middle School in the summer of 1945, Takikawa heard Emperor Hirohito's radio speech that, in effect, announced that Japan had lost the war. "All the adults were crying, but the children did not know what it was about," Takikawa recalls. "The radio was making scratchy sounds, so we couldn't make it out at all." He remains impressed that Japan managed to keep going, "Looking back on it now, I think that the Japanese people are really something. Even in the chaotic times right after the war, the milk was delivered reliably in those places that were not burned out, and street cars and railroads were running. At the time, I took those things as a matter of course."

His father, finally home, was unemployed, so young

Takikawa grabbed whatever temporary jobs he could find in Tokyo. At 17, he worked as a day laborer, clearing debris left by air raids, and also as a messenger, tutor, and hotel room boy. Takikawa got through high school by working afternoons and nights at the Ambassador Hotel, where he also served as a doorman and bartender.

Learning to part amicably from employers showed him that even a maverick can survive with a little diplomacy. As he puts it, "Here in Japan, people feel uncomfortable even walking by a company that has fired them. I had to leave in such a way that I could pass by any time, or else there would be no path left for me in Tokyo. You really have to be very careful not to burn your bridges."

As a Tokyo University student, Takikawa finally found a steady job and intellectual stimulation at the Japan-France Institute, an educational organization financed by the French government. Cut off from Western culture during the war, Takikawa eagerly went there to read French novels in translation and to see French movies. He acquired an enduring belief in the political essence of the French Revolution, which Japan has yet to put into practice fully: Sovereignty primarily rests with the people. Takikawa's diligence as a part-time accountant for the institute made a lasting impression on friends. He had a way of stepping in and solving problems. Once, the regular full-time accountant quit suddenly, leaving the books incomplete. Takikawa, then about 20 years old, took the original receipts and ledgers home, apparently worked through the night, and returned the next day with perfectly balanced accounts.

A LEADER WHO NEVER SEEMED TO STUDY

Says Shuji Takashina, a classmate who also worked at the Japan-France Institute and is now director-general of the

National Museum of Western Art in Tokyo, "Takikawa was so bright and cheerful that people clustered around him. He made a point of inviting us to his house—in essence, acting like a leader. He had a facade of not studying, but his grades were so good that we suspected otherwise."

Upon graduating from university, Takikawa figured that Canon, a young company with few senior executives, offered the best prospects for fast promotion. But he hated the work at first. Assigned to the welfare section of the personnel department, Takikawa spent two frustrating years doing menial chores, such as setting up tables and chairs for company celebrations, but tried to make the best of it. Recalls Takikawa, "I really wondered why I, and I alone, should apply iodine tincture to the arms of girls with cuts or carry tables, while others who had entered the company at the same time were attached to nifty sections like planning." To relieve his boredom, Takikawa persuaded Canon's management to let him start a company newsletter for which he was the entire staff.

His first boss Tomomasa Matsui saw Takikawa as "intelligent and yet like a ky*okaku*"—literally, a member of an organized gamblers' group—because of his forcefulness. Strange as it may seem, that was a compliment. In those days, the Japanese viewed their equivalent of a *mafioso* as a ruggedly romantic figure, says Matsui, "like the American cowboy." Historically, *kyokaku* were known for protecting the weak and attacking the strong. Noticing a streak of idealism in the young recruit, his supervisor encouraged Takikawa to get involved with the company union.

FIGHTING WITH UNION AGITATORS

Takikawa joined the labor organization to fill his idle time but discovered that it was a battlefield. In the immediate postwar years, communist ideologues—a vocal minority—sought to take over Japanese unions, including the one at Canon. Says Takikawa, "My fate was to fight them. The union needed someone who could control those radical activists—with logic." In heated meetings, some leftist organizers confronted Takikawa by asking, "What party do you belong to?" His reply was, "The Canon Party." Ultimately, Takikawa convinced most members to focus on improving pay and working conditions rather than on worrying about politics.

In 1961, he was elected to head the union, a full-time job, and became embroiled in another confrontation. Radical agitators campaigned to organize a separate union for some 1,500 part-time women employees, half the factory work force. Canon had hired the extra workers to keep up with demand for the Canonet, Japan's first compact 35 mm camera with an electric eye, but paid them less than regular employees. The part-timers staged daily demonstrations that grabbed attention of the media and left senior executives befuddled over what to do. "Facing 1,500 angry women is scary," says Takikawa, who spent three months trying to placate them. He boldly promised to provide the part-timers with equal status to other employees, then had to negotiate with management to gain acceptance of the idea.

His solution to the labor strife included a clever technique for weeding out the radical activists from the union. Immediately, some 60 percent of the part-timers were given formal examinations to obtain permanent status. Every three months thereafter, the remaining 40 percent of those employees had the opportunity to take similar exams. The agitators, who took jobs mainly to get inside Canon's union, eventually accepted the peaceful solution. Takikawa wound up a hero to both the workers and Canon's senior executives.

Still, Takikawa knew that he was taking a risk. As he tells it now, "In Japan, if you've been involved in a labor union for as long as four years, as I was, your chances of getting promoted usually are very small. The more successful I was with the union, the more decisively disadvantageous it seemed to my career." His union exploits, however, earned the admiration of Dr. Takeshi Mitarai, the company's founder and, in those days, its president.

In 1962, Dr. Mitarai selected Takikawa, at the time just 31, to manage the company's personnel department. Having stepped down from his union post only a year earlier, he was happily working in the marketing department—and resisted the promotion. Takikawa worried about switching roles and having to deal with the employees from management's side of the table. But his experience as a labor leader is precisely what appealed to Dr. Mitarai, who admired young men who had the courage of their convictions.

THE TALKING BOOK THAT FAILED

Certainly, Takikawa never hesitated to speak his mind. As a junior staffer in the marketing department, he blew the whistle on a product that Canon introduced with much fanfare: *Syncro Reader*, a kind of talking book that used magnetic material on the back of its pages and bulky equipment to produce sound. Though Syncro Reader failed miserably in the market, no one wanted to take responsibility for killing it. Takikawa, asked for his view of the product by a senior executive, spent two hours explaining that an ordinary book and an inexpensive tape recorder would do the same thing as the Syncro Reader. Finally, Canon withdrew the product.

His forcefulness, however, sometimes landed Takikawa

in trouble. As head of the labor union during tense negotiations, he gained the privilege of walking right into Dr. Mitarai's office anytime without an appointment. Soon after becoming personnel manager, Takikawa barged in during a meeting, and senior executives angrily chided him for bad manners. Dr. Mitarai calmed them down. Recalls Takikawa, "He gave me the grace to escape that day, but I never did that again."

As personnel manager, Takikawa found that union members still sought his advice when their organization got entangled in an internal struggle. Forbidden by law from getting directly involved, he met with colleagues in the union over drinks after working hours. "I took two of them out each night, meeting them one at a time at different bars," says Takikawa. He helped keep the peace, but ended up getting a stomach ulcer.

After a long night of drinking *sake*, Takikawa usually splurged on a taxi to the office the next morning. He befriended a cab driver, who worried that the young man would go broke taking a taxi to work and offered him a ride every day for a reasonable monthly fee. Takikawa, who was spending about one-third of his salary on cab fares, eagerly accepted the deal. "Thanks to that cab driver called Kagono," he says, "I could perform the miracle of reaching my office at 7:30 sharp every morning." This minor miracle was imperative. Dr. Mitarai, who arrived shortly thereafter each day, expected his personnel manager to be there waiting for him.

A LOTTERY LED TO MARRIAGE

Totally absorbed in his work, Takikawa even found his wife at Canon. Teruko, who joined the personnel department as a lively woman of 18, caught his eye. When they first met, he recalls, "I did not have concrete thoughts about marriage, but, in retrospect, maybe it was in the back of my mind." Their courtship was almost subliminal until four years later, when Takikawa unexpectedly won a lottery to obtain an apartment in a government housing project. Only then did he learn that bachelors were ineligible. Takikawa immediately turned to Teruko, who happened to be sitting in his office, and proposed marriage. "The apartment was not the only reason," says Takikawa, "but it brought us together fast."

(Now they have three sons and a weekend house on the Izu peninsula, where Takikawa brings mountains of paperwork. Says he, "My wife used to complain that 'I'm not married to a company.' She was absolutely right." Takikawa, in fact, seems to spend more time with his spouse than most high-powered Japanese executives.)

LEARNING ABOUT BUSINESS ABROAD

In 1966, Dr. Mitarai sent Takikawa around the world in 70 days, an extraordinary trip for a young manager in a country with little foreign exchange. Canon's president wanted a comprehensive plan for compensating employees, one that reflected the best international practices. Takikawa took off with $2,000 (the maximum a Japanese was then allowed to take abroad) and went to 17 countries—from Singapore to Europe and the United States. Every day, he visited at least two companies to study their personnel practices, and every night, he explored the pleasures of each city. "I may have drunk in every bar along the Rhine River," says Takikawa. He even wedged in side trips to Brazil (where his stepmother had a relative) and Hawaii, where his money ran out.

The trip proved to be an eye-opener for Takikawa. "I'm beginning to understand that the world is not so simple," he confessed in a perceptive article for Canon's in-house news-letter. The variety of life experiences (drab comrades in East Berlin, beatniks in San Francisco, Chinese refugees in Hong Kong) impressed him as much as visiting Xerox and Eastman Kodak. The inability of Japanese (including himself) to communicate well in English bothered Takikawa, who made friends by singing with people in bars. He discovered another universal language, money. As he tells it, "A dollar tip could get an American taxi driver to invite me to sit in the front and guide me through San Francisco in an English spoken as if he were talking to a child. And it could get a waiter in Geneva to show me the way to Canon's office." His world tour converted Takikawa into an ardent internationalist who, at the time, said, "What we Japanese need is not to be intimidated, not to be arrogant or boastful, but to work actively on the world stage."

Back in Tokyo, Dr. Mitarai castigated him for visiting Hawaii and Brazil, as well as for his drinking tour of the Rhine. But after reading—and approving—Takikawa's recommendations, the moralistic company president remarked, "This report shows that you did some work as well." What Takikawa discovered on his trip, in fact, changed Canon's entire approach to compensation, introducing merit pay increases in a system that had mainly rewarded people on the basis of seniority. Many other Japanese companies now emulate the Canon system: Employees can win promotions by exams up to a point, after which promotions depend on their job performance.

AMERICA, OPPORTUNITY OF A LIFETIME

Offered the presidency of Canon U.S.A. in 1970, Takikawa hesitated because that subsidiary had little responsibility. Since American companies handled the marketing of

Canon's products, Takikawa told his mentor, going to the United States was pointless. "If that's the way you feel," replied Dr. Mitarai, "why don't you go there and change things to your liking?" Canon's founder, according to Takikawa, also said, "If I were younger, I'd do the job myself—and not give you the chance."

President Mitarai, in fact, shrewdly maneuvered Takikawa into confirming his own instinctive view that the company needed to develop sales prowess. Canon was turning out innovative products, but suffered from weak marketing. In the American market, Canon was practically invisible. Its copiers and calculators were sold under the brand names of U.S. distributors, while Bell & Howell served as the exclusive sales agent for Canon cameras. Building his own sales organization in America appealed to Takikawa, he admits now, as "a once-in-a-lifetime opportunity."

Still, he boldly set other conditions for taking the job: Takikawa insisted on the power to make all decisions affecting the North American market and to recruit anyone at Canon to help him. Ordinarily, no Japanese manager would dare to negotiate terms for accepting an assignment from his boss, but Takikawa had developed a special relationship with Canon's president. Explains Takikawa, "My accomplishments in the labor union and the personnel department created a small legend, so Dr. Mitarai usually allowed me to do what I wanted." Besides, Dr. Mitarai agreed that no one could succeed in the United States without full authority.

To begin his new challenge in America, Takikawa arrived in New York in December 1970 with great hopes. He found that his crew at Canon U.S.A., however, was totally demoralized. Recalls Takikawa, "The 30 Japanese employees were at each other's throats and constantly preoccupied with the mood of their bosses in Tokyo. While they fought, the American employees looked on with amusement." Administering shock treatment, Takikawa ordered the Japanese to quit fighting each other and to take out their frustrations by denouncing the executives in Tokyo—who would not hear them anyway. The Japanese soon began acting more like members of a team.

WINNING OVER EMPLOYEES IN NEW YORK BARS

Ten days after he began, Takikawa delivered another jolt by telling his employees, "I want you to know that I won't listen to what Tokyo says for the next three years. Even if we succeed, I may get the boot. So if you want to go home, you may do so now." No one wanted to leave, especially since Canon U.S.A. was becoming an exciting place to work. To boost morale, Takikawa invited small groups of employees to piano bars in New York City. Recalls one participant of those sing-along nights: "People of our generation do not know Japanese military songs, the best morale-builders, but we learned them in New York bars."

Some of his troops even began expecting miracles. Hiroto Kagami, a manager with previous U.S. experience and a Takikawa recruit, spent many nights with his boss planning Canon's assault on the American market. Perhaps there are some shortcuts, Kagami suggested over a drink one evening. Takikawa turned very serious and said, "There is no such thing as a shortcut in business. The only way to beat your competitors is putting all your energy into it." At the time, Kagami, a friend and admirer of Takikawa, calculated his chances of success at about 50 percent.

Indeed, Takikawa encountered nothing but headaches initially. Bell & Howell was shocked to learn that the supposedly powerless president of Canon U.S.A. could cancel an exclusive distribution arrangement for cameras. Attempting to go around him, Bell & Howell approached Canon's Tokyo headquarters and proposed a U.S.-Japanese joint venture to distribute the cameras. Takeo Maeda, the Canon Inc. vice-president in charge of marketing, wanted to accept the offer. The Tokyo headquarters dithered over the matter for nearly six months. Finally, in December 1971, Takikawa, who had gotten wind of the discussions with Bell & Howell, flew home and hinted at the possibility of resigning from the U.S. job if he could not market Canon's products independently. (In the subtle Japanese society, even a gentle hint of that kind conveys a strong message.) Maeda exploded in anger, but eventually gave in. Dr. Mitarai, as always, left the gritty details to his subordinates, but ultimately Canon's board backed Takikawa.

Without waiting for that official approval, he had already started setting up a network of Canon sales offices in America—on borrowed funds. Selling Canon calculators to U.S. retailers was about the only thing that Takikawa's troops could do immediately. Monroe, the old U.S. distributor, was phasing out at his request. Eager to rev up sales fast, Takikawa ran into resistance from a small group of retailers known as master dealers. They were supposed to line up other dealers for Canon calculators in exchange for commissions, but did little with the franchise. Takikawa decided that Canon could sell a lot more calculators by expanding the number of retail outlets and abolishing the master-dealer system. Inevitably, his move displeased the master dealers.

SCREAMING AND SHOUTING U.S. DEALERS

While most Japanese shy away from conflicts, Takikawa staged a confrontation by inviting nearly 100 of those unhappy master dealers to a Long Island, New York, conference center. After two days of fruitless discussions, Takikawa, shaking in frustration, stood up and in his ragged English told the master dealers, "I came to this country to make Canon U.S.A. the distributor for all of our products. Unless we greatly increase sales of calculators, we will not be able to generate the funds necessary to build a sales organization for cameras and copiers. And I will have to resign. If I have to leave anyway, I'm going to abolish our calculator business in the United States—starting today. From the bottom of my heart, thanks for your sales efforts." He walked out, leaving the dealers screaming and shouting. After calming down, they gave in to Takikawa and continued selling Canon calculators. His tactics, though, could have backfired, possibly alienating American retailers. In retrospect, he says, "It was the kind of serious bout where you really bet your life."

Taking over copiers from Saxon, the U.S. distributor, turned out to be almost as stormy for Takikawa. The final negotiations in 1974 grew so tense that Canon's headquarters in Tokyo ordered him to stay away from Saxon. "Saying that was one thing," remarks Takikawa, "but removing me from the negotiations caused a lot of inconvenience." Without disobeying Tokyo, Takikawa kept up with the state of play by meeting regularly with a Saxon vice-president—at a Manhattan coffee shop.

Takikawa encountered more difficulties in obtaining paper with just the right characteristics for Canon copiers. Selling machines without it was unthinkable to him, but American suppliers could not be lined up in time. So Takikawa went to a paper factory in Kangas, Finland, about 280 miles north of Helsinki—and had a wonderful time. Between negotiations, he discovered the delights of sauna baths and the joys of drinking through nights that never turn dark in summer. But in the fall, just before the U.S. launch of Canon copiers, Takikawa received dismal news: His paper—tons of it—still had not been shipped. He ordered that it be sent by plane at great expense. Remarks Takikawa, "I really had to pay for the great fun we had in Finland with all that sauna and white night. The copiers were introduced on time and profitably, but we lost a small fortune on that paper."

A $2 MILLION GAMBLE ON TV ADS

Selling cameras solidly established Takikawa's reputation in America. After Bell & Howell handed over its inventory in the summer of 1973, Takikawa spent several weekends helping his staff repackage the cameras in fancy new boxes. From the start, his team outpaced the sales volume of the former American distributor. But his breakthrough came in 1976, when Canon introduced the AE-1, the first single lens reflex camera that was computerized and, thus, easy to use. Rather than marketing this camera only to serious photographers, Takikawa pushed it as a mass consumer item. He invested about $2 million, his entire company's profits for the year, in U.S. network television commercials—another first for Japanese cameras. "It was a gamble," says Takikawa. "Almost no one in Canon U.S.A. agreed with me, but it was my decision." His move paid off handsomely. Sales zoomed up to more than 50,000 per month, 10 times more than Bell & Howell ever did for Canon.

The surge of consumer interest enabled Canon to forego rebates to dealers, which are commonly offered by Japanese manufacturers. "Suddenly, we had a three-month backlog of orders," recalls Takikawa. "I had to travel to Japan every month to make sure that shipments would be coming by air freight." This reinforced his view that Canon could sell more of its products by investing in promotion rather than discounts.

His TV commercials stimulated so much demand, in fact, that many American consumers could not find Canon AE-1 cameras in stores and, instead, bought other Japanese brands. Pentax and Minolta managers in the United States even threw a party to thank Takikawa, who says, "That's the only time that I've ever heard words of gratitude from competitors." Unnoticed amid the excitement over that camera, he also managed to sell Canon equipment to all three American TV networks that year.

To his relief, hot camera sales in 1976 enabled Takikawa to pay off the $30 million debt that he accumulated in opening sales offices. Suddenly, he was popular with Japanese bank managers in New York, who had irritated him earlier by demanding loan guarantees from Canon's Tokyo headquarters. He had pointedly told them that Canon U.S.A. could borrow from American banks without such guarantees. Most Japanese executives in America tended to refer even routine matters to their home offices in Japan, so those Japanese bankers never quite appreciated the extent of Takikawa's authority.

THE "GODFATHER" FROM JAPAN

His American employees, however, nicknamed Takikawa the "Godfather" because he could make decisions and act quickly without consulting Tokyo. To compensate for limited fluency in English, Takikawa consciously strived to be what he terms "the Japanese president who always does what he says he will do." He also gained the respect of American employees and minimized the language barrier by always keeping in his head the exact sales figures for every product.

In just six years, Takikawa accomplished a goal that was to have taken a decade, boosting sales of Canon U.S.A.

from $15 million to over $200 million annually. (He laid a solid foundation; and, by 1992, Canon U.S.A. generated sales of $4 billion—one-third the Canon Group's total revenues.) Dr. Mitarai, who set the original timetable for Takikawa and never believed in handing out compliments frivolously, told his protégé, "It's expected that you do good work. Now you should work on polishing up your character." For once, the usually outspoken Takikawa could think of no response. As he now says, "Improving your character is an endless process. Who can say that he has a perfect character?"

His reward was an even more daunting job, marketing Canon's products in Japan. In 1977, Takikawa became president of Canon Sales Co., a subsidiary with 1,500 employees—but no one selling directly to end-users. Canon Sales in those days was principally a wholesaler that lacked contact with the customers actually using its machines. He started direct sales with an organization of only 14 people to sell copiers throughout the country, while Xerox and Ricoh deployed as many as 2,000 salesmen in the city of Tokyo alone. Recalls Takikawa, "Our guys were intimidated by the competition. I really felt pity for them." He rallied employees with the vision of building a marketing company so potent that it could be floated on the stock exchange.

Takikawa chose a dramatic moment to reveal his ambitions. He invited 30 presidents of leading Japanese office-equipment dealers to the United States. They landed in New York on July 13, 1977—the night of a sudden power failure. It struck while Takikawa was hosting a dinner in Manhattan, but he went on exchanging toasts with Japanese dealers. Candlelight gave the party a festive atmosphere, as Takikawa outlined a grand design for dominating the Japanese copier market: Any dealer that sold 70 copiers a month would belong to a special Canon club and

receive incentives like overseas trips; with 100 such dealers, Canon could triple its market share to 30 percent. "It
was a dream," says one dealer who attended the dinner.
"But under the influence of alcohol, we all cheered."

A NIGHT EVERYONE REMEMBERS

What sold the dealers on making Takikawa's dream a reality was sharing the rigors of the Manhattan blackout over
the next 20 hours. Takikawa led the group through pitch-
dark streets to the darkened Americana Hotel, where both
elevators and air-conditioning were not working. The Japanese dealers, who had heard in Tokyo about the perils of
crime in Manhattan, began fearing the worst. But Takikawa
took care of them. He assigned a young subordinate with a
bunch of candles to walk all the guests to their rooms—on
the 38th floor and above. (Takikawa, who had reserved a
suite on the 47th floor, had the longest walk.) Early the next
morning, the city was still without electricity. Takikawa
phoned his former staffers at Canon U.S.A. in Long Island
(which had normal power), and ordered them to bring food
to the Americana Hotel. After a brunch of *onigiri* (rice balls
stuffed with such things as pickled plum or salmon), he took
the dealers to Long Island, ending the mild adventure.

The blackout, however, assumed heroic stature in the
minds of those Canon dealers. Most Japanese get very
uneasy about anything unexpected—especially when there's
a whiff of potential danger. Says Yoshiyuki Todaka, the
Canon manager who reassuringly escorted anxious guests
up the dark stairways, "That was an epoch-making evening,
creating a real bond between the dealers and Takikawa—
like soldiers united against a common enemy." Todaka
even wrote postcards to the wives of Canon's guests report-

ing that their husbands were fine. He won a promotion from Takikawa, along with the enduring nickname "staircase general manager."

It took Takikawa 15 years to attain supremacy for Canon copiers, an achievement that he celebrated by taking dealers on another trip. At a cost of some $3 million, Takikawa hosted a party of 230 people—dealers and their wives—on a grand junket to Paris and Nice in May 1992. Takikawa told his guests that the big blackout in New York "was indeed a strange occasion for the start of this great challenging task, and a rather fitting one, I think." Even in Paris, the shared experience of the blackout was still a unifying force for Takikawa and the Japanese dealers.

His methods of winning a top market share, however, had already tested the loyalty of dealers. In 1978, he set up Canon Eiken to sell products directly to consumers and to train salespeople. Initially, Takikawa's creation looked like a direct competitor to independent dealers, several of whom (he recalls) asked him, "Are you trying to destroy us?" He spent much time convincing retailers that everyone would benefit from an additional sales channel: His team concentrated on customers no one else served, and its experience would enable Canon to improve support to the dealers. Later, in fact, their sons and successors came to Canon Eiken for training. Says Takikawa, "I had learned from the United States that opening new sales channels causes trouble with existing dealers—and demands much patient explanation."

PUSHING SALESMEN TO GET OUT AND SELL

Remolding attitudes of his own employees was just as demanding. Takikawa assigned his company's best salespeople to Canon Eiken, which other executives took to calling sarcastically "the royal domain of the president." His personal involvement, however, made a crucial difference. During the early days of Canon Eiken, Takikawa dropped by a meeting of senior managers, who were busily listing their problems on a blackboard. He exploded in anger, saying, "You're crazy. We can't afford to sit around for three days discussing difficulties. Get out, go see customers." His outburst reminded managers to lead by accompanying salesmen on their rounds, rather than simply talking with each other.

Eventually, Canon Eiken expanded its ranks from 14 to 2,000 salespeople, who avoided what Takikawa describes as "the big-company disease" by always trying something new. (The Japanese word *Eiken*, in fact, connotes an organization that develops new marketing techniques.) This sales force, for example, works in teams of five—each headed by a salesman in his mid-twenties who has performed well. Whenever the Japanese economy slows down, as it has in the past few years, Takikawa trims overheads of such departments as finance and personnel by shifting some of their employees into Canon Eiken. Having them out calling on customers, of course, bolsters sales.

ACQUIRING NEW COMPANIES

To extend the reach of Canon Sales Co., Takikawa also acquired several ailing Japanese companies and took their salesmen into his fold. In 1979, Copyer Co. failed with its own outdated copying machines, and its 60 sales offices, as Takikawa puts it, "rolled into my lap." Likewise, a year later, he absorbed a computer sales company called Nippon Elex and, in 1985, Nippon Typewriter. Taking over corporations is touchy in Japan, where employees traditionally feel that they belong to a particular firm. Takikawa won their loyalty by treating his acquisitions like members of the Canon family and avoiding mass layoffs. The turnover rate among his employees—now totaling some 9,000—is a low 4 percent a year.

Takikawa motivates his relatively young sales force by making marketing, as he puts it, "fun and interesting." His key subordinates are almost as iconoclastic as Takikawa. Tohru Kaneko, 51, now a senior executive, is a renegade from the Japanese Finance Ministry, which he quit after a couple of dull years spent compiling customs statistics. Seeking excitement, Kaneko joined the crew of a U.S. Navy merchant ship that supplied Vietnam in 1967. "I was curious about the war," he says, "and wanted to test my guts." Kaneko lasted only six months but came away with a lesson that serves him well at Canon Sales: "Without the mind of a missionary, you can lose even with first-class equipment." Still, it took him three months at Canon before he could learn to sell anything, and then the sheer joy of being able to do it helped make Kaneko a star. Says he of Takikawa, "He doesn't want to hear what someone has done in the past, but what he will do in the future."

APPLE COMPUTER'S TIMELY PITCH

Steady profits from copying machines enabled Takikawa to diversify into computers, even though Canon makes few of them. In 1983, Takikawa jumped at the chance to become the exclusive sales agent for Apple computers in Japan, an opportunity that he terms "a gift from heaven." Apple's offer came just as Takikawa was preparing to launch a unique chain of retail shops featuring computers and software. This fit perfectly into his master plan for obtaining an independent listing on the Tokyo stock exchange. To qualify, at least 30 percent of his company's business had to be completely unrelated to the parent corporation, Canon Inc. Takikawa did that largely by selling American products, starting with equipment for making semiconductors and winding up with eight brands of U.S. computers.

Takikawa's retail stores gave Japan something different and provided him with a flashy way to boost sales. His nearly 100 Zero-One shops are the most computer-friendly places in Japan. Consumers can try out the latest products, obtain training, get machines serviced, and—of course—buy computers. "The Macintosh is like a Chinese panda in a zoo, drawing people into our shops," says a Zero-One manager in Tokyo. The innovative retail outlets have produced results that surprised even Takikawa: Making computers attractive and accessible to individual consumers also attracted corporate buyers, which now account for 70 percent of sales. Takikawa lost no time in staffing each store with two separate sales forces, one for consumers who walk in and another that specializes in serving companies. And he appointed women as assistant managers in shops, a departure from the male-dominated Japanese business world.

His link with Apple, however, had some rough moments. Canon Sales Co. lost its exclusive franchise for Apple in Japan after just three years. Apple was ending such arrangements everywhere as part of its global strategy, but Takikawa argued that it was unfair. He had invested heavily in promoting Apple computers for profits that had yet to materialize. An executive of the American computer company, however, reminded Takikawa that, as president of Canon U.S.A., he, too, had canceled exclusive distribution contracts to further a broader strategy. "He touched at a samurai's most vulnerable point," acknowledges Takikawa, who is still the biggest Japanese distributor of Apple computers and, he says, "the world's largest Macintosh retailer." As a result of his success with U.S. products, IBM has enlisted Takikawa to sell its machines in his shops, too.

Once more, his achievements initially won little praise from Dr. Mitarai. In August 1981, when Takikawa gained a listing for Canon Sales Co. on the second tier of the Tokyo exchange, Dr. Mitarai, then chairman, remarked, "This is like prep school for becoming an outstanding company, so don't let it go to your head." A year and 10 months later, Takikawa made it into the first section of the stock exchange and wondered what his mentor would say. Dr. Mitarai surprised him with unqualified praise saying, "You have really done well." So unusual was the compliment that Canon executives wondered if something might be wrong with the chairman. A year later, Dr. Mitarai, at the age of 83, died of cancer.

Now, Takikawa is trying to give his own young employees the opportunity to be creative upstarts, too. He has started an unusual program that encourages new recruits to voice their opinions freely and to try new approaches to their jobs. Under what Takikawa calls "the brother system," groups of 10 new recruits are assigned a couple of mentors who have been with Canon for three years. The mentors get an allowance to socialize outside the office with the newcomers—and listen to their gripes and ideas. As Takikawa likes to say, "Our company reflects the vitality of youth."

In short, he believes that Canon—and Japan—need mavericks. Says Takikawa, "Once you make a series of legendary accomplishments, group consensus no longer applies. Instead, people tend to say, *that* man is different, unusual. He can do what he wants, and chances are that he will succeed."

4

A Preview of Canon's Twenty-First Century

Canon should set its sights on long-selling products rather than short-term best sellers...A long-seller offers unprecedented originality so that competitors will need time to close the gap. In short, a long-seller is a genuine market leader and incorporates a real breakthrough in its essential function.

—*Canon's strategic plan*

 acsimile machines that transmit full-color images. An eye-controlled camera that focuses on any point at which the user is looking when the shutter release is pressed (infrared beams in the camera detect the angle at which the eye is turned). Thin display screens for computers. The world's lightest and smallest fax machine—just 2.2 pounds, about the size of a book, and able to be plugged into a pay phone. Efficient solar cells that generate electricity at reasonable cost.

These are not dream products but innovations Canon showed off at a traveling exhibit that reached New York in March 1993. Besides gaining glimpses of Canon's future, visitors to the Canon Tech Expo could try out many of the products and watch others in operation. Displaying works in progress was, in effect, a strong statement of the company's confidence in its technology.

Simultaneously, Canon started another move to shape its future, what the company terms a "rejuvenation" of its senior management. New presidents in their fifties have been appointed to key companies in the Canon Group, while their predecessors remain very much on the scene. Giving more responsibility to a younger generation of leaders is, of course, part of the Canon culture.

Changes affect the top levels of the parent company.

Dr. Keizo Yamaji, a Ph.D. engineer and president of Canon Inc. for four years, has moved up to vice-chairman. Says Dr. Yamaji, who also became chairman of Canon U.S.A. and Canon Europe, "I want to further the globalization of Canon. I'd like to put my effort into quicker and more successful activities of Canon's overseas research-and-development facilities so that they can provide fruit as early as possible." His successor as president is another technology specialist: Dr. Hajime Mitarai, son of the company's founder. A Ph.D. engineer from Stanford University, he joined Canon after working for the American company Corning.

LOOKING AT NEW COMPUTER SCREENS

Canon's technology gurus—who transformed a camera maker into a far broader image-and-information company—foresee continuing diversification. In devising new kinds of copying machines and printers, Canon researchers have come up with promising know-how that can be used in other fields. Among other things, Canon believes that it has *the* replacement for the bulky, eye-straining, cathode-ray-tube monitors still used today as computer screens. The company has developed Ferroelectric Liquid Crystal Display (FLC) for high-resolution flat-panel screens. Monochrome versions are being built for Canon's computer workstations in Japan, and 20-inch color versions will follow soon. Says Dr. Yamaji, "In this technology, we are at least five years ahead of other companies."

Another big Canon goal is to make solar energy cells a commercial product by the turn of the century. Technology for the amorphous silicon solar cell is derived from Canon's research on its high-speed copiers. To perfect the solar cell, Canon has formed joint ventures with two American companies, Plasma Physics and Energy Conversion Devices. Canon wants to combine the newest and best technologies, and then (in keeping with its corporate strategy of marketing products where they are invented) produce the cells in the United States.

Canon's marketing activities are also getting some rejuvenation. Takikawa has become chairman of Canon Sales Co. but remains chief executive and chief strategist for marketing in Japan. The new president, Hideharu Takemoto, previously headed Canon U.S.A. and worked under Takikawa long ago in Canon's personnel department. And the new president of Canon's American subsidiary is Haruo Murase, one of Takikawa's recruits for the U.S. operation 23 years ago.

Now that he has been elevated to chairman of Canon Sales in Japan, what will the maverick Takikawa do? Characteristically, he will defy the usual practice of having the company president serve as chief executive. Says Takikawa: "I intend to give daily routine responsibilities to Takemoto, and I will focus on group strategy for the eight subsidiaries (of which I am chairman) and that need a lot of hand-holding." In short, he does not intend to fade into the background and serve as an adviser, a common role for Japanese corporate chairmen. Remarks Takikawa, "I was looking forward to playing golf every day, but my scenario doesn't allow it."

A NEW UNIVERSE FOR A "SALES GOD"

Takikawa wants to nurture several of his smaller creations into high-powered sales arms for Canon in the next century. Canon Supercomputing, which he set up to sell Cray supercomputers and other scientific products, is one of his great hopes for selling both hardware and expertise. Already, he has proved that the real sales effort begins after a sale is made. Having installed a Cray supercomputer at the research center of a Tokyo construction company, Takikawa dispatched Canon engineers to provide what he describes as "deep hand-holding." This careful attention led to another sale of $800,000 in workstations.

Another little company that Takikawa likes is Alcantech, a joint venture between Canon Sales and Alcatel of France, which makes semiconductor manufacturing equipment that complements the Canon line. He remarks: "Its sales are about $40 million, not a big amount, but, at semiconductor trade shows, you can see that Alcantech products outnumber those of Canon in this area of materials manufacturing. By the twenty-first century, I expect this to be an important company."

Outside his company, Takikawa is devoting himself to distinctively Japanese educational pursuits. He manages Akita Institute of Computing and Accounting. Having worked his way through high school and encountered his own problems with exams, Takikawa can identify with the struggles of youth. He wants to offer a second chance for a career to thousands of Japanese who cannot get into a university. Their alternative is an institute like Akita. Remarks Takikawa, "At the age of 17 to 18, they try to realign themselves with society, but realize they cannot advance to higher education or get adequate employment."

Determined to add a new dimension to Japanese education, he is also helping the Computer Graphics Arts Society. It was conceived by both university professors and industry professionals—and organized by leading corporations: Canon Sales, NTT Data Communications, IBM Japan, and Nippon Electric Company. The Society promotes testing of the ability of Japanese to handle computer graphics,

which enables them to earn a national certificate, and encourages life-long learning for creative minds.

What excites Takikawa is that all of his activities build
up skills for systems integration, that is, making different
kinds of computers and peripheral equipment work together, which he sees as the future source of sales power for
Canon. Another force, of course, is Takikawa himself—as
can be seen from the ideas he unfolds in Part Two.

Part Two

Takikawa's Personal Recipes for Building Business

5

The Company President Must Be a Scenario Writer

I look at everything as a story. Every business enterprise has a history. In effect, I write the history before it happens. It must be a story that lasts for 10 to 20 years. Without longevity, or at least the potential for it, somewhere along the line the story will fail. There must be a continuous flow of events leading to an objective. The parts must fit together in more-or-less linear fashion. The scenario must not have back-and-forth action, but always move forward.

My idea of a scenario is much like that in the movie industry, However, here it defines where business actions take place. Generally, it tells who will say or do what to whom, but allows the individuals involved to decide the best ways to express it in a manner that suits the players and the business environment.

To unfold a story of entrepreneurial activity, one needs to back it up with people, things, and money. One of my favorite mottoes is: "Be strong with figures." I do not mean that a person has to become an expert in mathematics and computer science. But in starting a business project, one should be able to forecast future developments by firmly grasping the figures that form the scientific analysis and backing for the venture.

The first time that I developed a scenario in this fashion was when I assumed the presidency of Canon U.S.A. in 1970. Frankly, that company then was really little more than a mailbox, since Canon products were being distributed by American companies. Five people before me had failed at Canon U.S.A. No one in the Tokyo head office knew how to succeed in a foreign land.

Before accepting the job, I insisted on having the authority to take back distribution from American companies and make all decisions affecting North America. My boss, the late Chairman Dr. Takeshi Mitarai, agreed to those terms under one condition: Within 10 years, I would have to make the American subsidiary generate at least $100 million in annual sales of cameras, copiers, and calculators. That was quite a challenge. At the time, Canon U.S.A. had $15 million annual revenues, mostly from cameras sold exclusively by Bell & Howell. Canon calculators were handled by Monroe, and the copying machines by Saxon. As things turned out, I exceeded his target by creating a workable scenario.

I was just 39 years old, but I thought of the long-term need for Canon to establish its own sales channels. Therefore, I had to come up with a scenario for canceling distribution contracts with the three American companies, gradually and in sequence. We had to keep in mind the contractual terms requiring so much advance notice to the U.S. distributors—and then we had to turn around and handle those sales ourselves. Even my closest colleagues figured that I had only about a fifty-fifty chance of coming up with a scenario that would hold together.

Our U.S. operation in those days was very small—it had only about 50 employees—so there was no one else to create a scenario for me. Working on it day and night, including Saturdays and Sundays, I probably got into the habit of doing my own scenario writing. I even worked on it sitting in New York City bars.

In essence, we started by pushing sales of electronic calculators, raising cash to take over camera distribution from Bell & Howell, then finally moving on to copiers. Within six years, Canon U.S.A. had reached sales of $130 million.

The average Japanese chief executive often waits for recommendations and plans to well up from the bottom of the organization. The company may have someone write the scenario for the company president, who simply reads it. I feel that approach is probably unwise. Instead, I outline the scenario, get reactions to it, and make corrections—and then present the case. That way I have input from my subordinates and the benefit of two-way communication. There is no point in having a lot of discussion unless an idea can be developed into a story of ongoing business.

Ten years can produce results far beyond your hopes and dreams if you have a good scenario—a very clear vision that is forward-looking—along with scientific and sound planning. However, if you go through life with simple hopes and let days pass as if you are in a dream, then a decade will pass quickly without your having accomplished anything.

I am a take-charge type of person. Once I take responsibility for something, I picture various scenarios, racking my brain, thinking out how to turn an idea into a reality. The greatest pleasure of being a company president is having something work out as well as it was pictured in the scenario.

6

Make Marketing Fun and Interesting

9 had to make everyone enjoy marketing, the speciality of my company, or else we would not last very long. Somehow our work had to become fun and interesting—as we say in Japanese, *omoshiroi*. My first clue came from a dictionary, which defines that word not only as something delightful, bright, and enjoyable, but also as something that opens up a horizon. I thought long and hard about how to make marketing a means to open horizons for employees. The concept sounds great, but it is not so simple to do. And yet my business scenario for the 1990s is based on that idea.

What does it take? When I really looked at it, the people inside the company were mostly salesmen who constantly ran around calling on customers—with quotas that seem to increase year by year. What is fun about that? How does that open up horizons? I decided that one way would be to create new tactics, new products and services, new strategies to make sales with more ease.

One change made the lives of both our salesmen and our customers more exciting by establishing a chain of nearly 100 Zero-One shops that sell computers and related equipment. Salesmen who used to get worn out and bored making endless sales calls now bring clients into our shops to demonstrate products.

As the famous Japanese writer Soseki Natsume pointed out, "The greater the joy, the greater the suffering is bound to be." We know that easy work, however, is generally too commonplace, monotonous, and boring. I wanted my staff to get enough joy to make a sustained effort.

To make marketing more *omoshiroi*, we must come up with easy-to-understand project themes that will broaden and lighten the space before the eyes of our employees, the kind of themes on which our people can work enthusiastically and enjoyably. The atmosphere must encourage experimenting to clarify things that we do not yet understand and to take up challenges without being afraid of failures.

The entrepreneurial spirit makes our lives more interesting. That idea came out of my thinking that we should be able to find limitless joy in the vitality that creates new work.

Since I myself push out ideas one after another, I want to see all of our people come up with and present ideas as well. As was true in the age of rising capitalism, I am always hoping and praying that we can create a laissez-faire corporate ethos in which everyone actively tries to do new things. I tell people, "Do not be afraid of failing, but never repeat the same failure twice. Otherwise, no matter how much money we have, it won't be adequate."

My plan for making the company more interesting boils down to three fundamental elements. First, I decided that just selling the same old products day in and day out, chasing after a quota, is not going to be fun. So I had to give insights into the future. My goal is to transform a trading firm into a systems integrator of graphic images and information. That is a high-tech description, but the idea is really not complex. In essence, we will solve business problems for our customers not by selling them a single Canon product, but a combination of hardware and software from various manufacturers. This will bring new products, new technologies, new ways of selling.

My second element for making marketing more interesting is to understand and embrace globalization. Our employees had always viewed Canon Sales Co. as a purely local organization mainly because their charter was sales and marketing in Japan. But I wanted to impress upon them that this is not the case. The Canon Group is very strong in digital imaging devices and technologies, but not in computers. We have to import computer capabilities, so our employees should be the vanguard who bring new ideas and products into the country. And by combining them with Canon products, we can have good integrated systems—and, thus, serve in a global fashion. Canon Inc., our parent corporation, exports products around the world, but its efforts probably will be frowned upon as trade problems with other countries deteriorate. My company's imports of American computers are one means of easing international trade frictions.

Thirdly, giving the staff more vacation time makes everyone more enthusiastic about work. Starting in 1989, I introduced what Canon Sales Co. calls a free vacation system. Our parent company, Canon Inc., takes a two-week vacation in the summer. However, we could not have two continuous weeks of summer vacation without hearing complaints from our customers. So the decision was made to create free vacations. One week would be in the summer when everyone in Japan takes some vacation. The other week (actually nine days, if you include Saturdays and Sundays) is taken at any other time an employee chooses, provided that it does not affect work commitments.

In addition, there is still more time off under a system called refreshing holidays. Instead of awarding watches or other gifts to employees after a certain number of years in the company, I give them extra vacation days. Here is how it works: After the first five years of continuous service, employees get an extra three days of vacation. In the tenth year, they get an extra two weeks. When the free vacation time and the refreshing time are combined, workers can take a maximum of 23 paid days off during the year. That is in addition to regular vacations of a minimum 12 days.

The ultimate intent of this vacation policy is to change the habits of Japanese, who are typically poor users of vacations. This encourages them to take an extended family vacation (which is still rare in our country) or to go off on a real sabbatical. In other Japanese companies, many employees somehow feel that it is disloyal to use all of their paid holidays, but I try to set an example by always taking my full vacation. Our people should start thinking about additional leisure and family time as a new way of Japanese life for the twenty-first century.

My vision is that everyone must learn well, work well, earn profits well—and play well.

7

My Secrets for Training Salesmen

The first thing salesmen need is self-confidence. For a start, the trick is to let them taste the benefits of winning. I usually assign easy-to-sell dealers and consumers to new salesmen so that they can taste the joy of receiving orders—and get accustomed to winning. Then salesmen can meet any potential customer bravely and perform at 120 percent of their supposed ability.

Sales competition is heavier in Japan than in the United States, but paying commissions to Japanese salesmen does not work well. At Canon, we tested the American commission system for several years about 25 years ago, but finally stopped it. Japanese employees did not like it. Japanese salesmen want at least 90 percent of their compensation to be a fixed salary, but American salespeople often prefer 20 percent salary and 80 percent commission. In Japan, not even the salesmen for IBM and Xerox are likely to get commissions.

In Japan, I have found more effective ways to motivate the sales force. Our best people are out meeting customers most of the day, rather than sitting around at the office. But I make a point of assigning every salesman his own desk. This gives them status and, more importantly, self-confidence.

Our biggest sales organization, Canon Eiken, operates in teams of five, each led by an experienced salesperson who looks after the problems of the other four sales people on the team. Traditionally, Japan gives emphasis to seniority, but we measure sales by performance. The group leader is not necessarily the oldest person but is the best performer—usually someone 26 or 27 years old with three to four years of experience. If there is too big a gap between the leader and his team, it does not work. Just selling more than others does not get reflected in compensation; a team leader gets only about $60 extra each month.

Openly ranking salesmen by their performance helps boost their efforts, too. I borrowed designations from the U.S. Army, such as three-star general and four-star general, to build a system for motivating retailers in Japan.

In 1979, I announced the founding of the Star Master Salesmen Association directed toward the salesmen of our dealers. Those who achieved the highest level sales target came to be called Five-Star Masters, followed by Four-Star Masters, Three-Star Masters, and so on.

The award ceremony for One- and Two-Star Masters is carried out at each branch around the country, while the ceremonies for Three-Star Masters and above status are carried out in one location as a national event. Today, outstanding salesmen of Three-Star and above number more than several hundred. At first, however, there were no Five-Star Masters.

In the friendly party after the first national Star Master Salesmen award-giving ceremony in 1981, I called out loudly, "Is there no General of the Army, no Five-Star General? Next year, I would really like to see even just one Five-Star General." Several hot-blooded, enthusiastic salesmen responded to my call, pledging to meet the goal in the following year.

Sure enough, at the award ceremony of 1982, 12 Five-Star Generals made their appearance. I was so glad of this that I invited them to come on board our company cruiser *Monte Cristo II*, which went at the full speed of 25 knots around the waters off Oshima Island. We had a really enjoyable day together—and that, too, strengthened the pride of our Five-Star Generals. Now, we have nearly 100 people a year become Five-Star Generals, so it is not so easy to hold an event for all them.

When we add up the number of dealer salesmen, plus salesmen of subsidiaries and our company itself, we have well over 10,000 salesmen for office equipment and machinery alone. Those salesmen are the precious treasure of our company.

I have even opened a private club in the Ginza, the entertainment district of Tokyo, as a sales incentive for dealers. This is called the 3,000 Club—meaning that membership is open to dealers who maintain 3,000 of our copiers in operation. The club has 70 members, whose names are engraved on a board at the entrance. This gives dealers a lot of prestige, especially when they bring clients or employees into the 3,000 Club. And drinking there is vastly cheaper than anywhere else of its kind in Japan.

As we build sales power, of course, the volume of our company's sales has steadily risen. More importantly, our vow to win a leading share in the plain-paper copier market of Japan has been realized. We have gone from barely 10 percent to a 30 percent share. It took 15 years to accomplish this feat, but it all began with building up the self-confidence of every salesman.

8

A New Sales Era Is Dawning

his is an era in which real sales activity begins *after* you make a sale. This concept may seem like a mysterious aphorism, but it is a very basic idea—and essential for sustaining any sales effort.

The first and foremost meaning of this concept is that once the sale is closed for a copier product, I would like to sell a facsimile machine, word processor, computer, or camera to the same customer. I call this situation *Canon on Canon*, selling an additional Canon product to someone who has already purchased one.

This concept has a second meaning, which I call *Canon to Canon*. Whenever Canon sells a copier, then the real sales effort starts for service, paper, toner, and even recycling. (We gather used cartridges and send them to a Canon plant in Dalian, China, for recycling.) Our salesmen also supply something else that is crucial—information service so that customers stay with Canon and within four or five years buy a new copier. Using these tactics, we sell the product, not letting competitors steal that customer away from us.

The Canon-to-Canon concept is very important. In Japan, we have 800,000 copiers in use today. If those copiers were replaced by products of competitors, this company would go bankrupt. On the other hand, it also pays to remember that the 800,000 users of Canon copiers are potential customers for Canon facsimile machines.

Salesmen who continue selling after making the initial sale are the cutting edge for marketing any product. The challenge, of course, is making sure that our salespeople have this attitude. I ask all employees to operate as if they were members of a think tank, a company that thrives on its ideas.

In the United States a think tank is made up of the best people in each field, and its clients pay top fees for ideas.

In Japan, there are a number of groups like think tanks, such as Nomura Research Institute, but the top people in each field do not join think tanks. They tend to stay at a university or a company.

I realize, of course, that our employees do not work quite like the intellectuals in a first-rate think tank. But I want all employees to think and create something, not spend their time doing the same thing the company has always done.

As a result, Canon people keep coming up with ideas for a new era of sales. During slow periods, we assign employees from one department (such as administration) to new sales channels—for example, selling 8 mm home-video camcorders (camera-recorders) to special stores that big Japanese corporations run for their employees. I call this my PKO, which in Japan stands for the peace-keeping operations of the United Nations. At Canon, *PKO* means something very different, our Profit-Keeping Operations.

Another of our PKO plans strengthens relations with businesses that own our copiers. Instead of just selling them paper, we are experimenting with a scheme that also picks up and hauls away their waste paper for recycling.

My biggest worry is that Canon might become afflicted with what I call "the big company disease," meaning that an organization becomes set in its ways and unimaginative. The best vaccine against the disease is to constantly come up with new ideas for selling to both old and new customers.

9

Even a Product That Fails Can Plant Seeds for Success

One of the best things that ever happened to me in business was getting involved early in my career in a commercial failure. This is not just philosophical rationalization. A product that consumers rejected taught me memorable lessons in marketing—and built relationships that benefit me even today.

At the age of 28, I was assigned to work on Canon's first attempt to diversify into office equipment. In May 1959, we generated much excitement in Japan by introducing a unique product called Syncro Reader, a talking book.

We marketed this new magnetic recording device in a grand way. It supposedly had many applications. You could use it to create a letter that would contain both written words and your voice. A Japanese book publisher produced foreign language lessons and children's books for the Syncro Reader. One newspaper even produced a tabloid that you could hear as well as read with our product. And a couple of brokerage houses used the Syncro Reader to lure customers by listing current stock quotes, while a voice discussed market trends.

At first, I was really absorbed in the idea of a book that produced sound. We had manufactured 2,000 Syncro Readers and sold nearly 1,000 of them in the first six months. But then no one wanted to buy the product. It just died.

Trying to figure out what was wrong with the Syncro Reader, I took one of them apart. It was a heavy thing, weighing about 20 pounds, a bulky device for doing a fairly simple job. The machine had three magnetic heads that scanned a magnetic strip on the back of ordinary paper to produce sound. It was really a recorder, not a reader. When I reassembled it, there were many pieces left over.

After a while, I figured out why no one wanted to buy this product. Magnetic-coated paper did not produce a stable sound. Probably the real killer was the fact that Syncro Reader could not be read in the comfortable style in which people perused a book. You always had to sit up, put the book on top of the Syncro Reader, and look down at it. That was the only position in which you could read and hear at the same time. When the tape recorder became more efficient and compact, we realized that having a textbook and listening to a tape recorder was far more efficient than the Syncro Reader.

Everyone involved with the Syncro Reader knew its eventual fate, but no one would come out in the open to suggest its termination. Dr. Takeshi Mitarai, who was then president of the company, was quite interested in the product and about 30 people really pushed it hard. Dohkan Ishihara, then the senior managing director and number two in Canon, once called me in and asked about a rumor he kept hearing—that the Syncro Reader project ought to be terminated. I was not even a manager, but that is one of the unusual things about the Canon organization. For two hours, I explained what had happened and why the project had to be terminated. No one would spend nearly $400 for dedicated equipment when you could do the same job for far less using a portable tape recorder and a book. I explained that the Syncro Reader, which had few practical applications, was really not a business.

Ishihara, who was very perceptive, immediately went to Dr. Mitarai and recommended that the program be terminated. Not only did Dr. Mitarai kill the Synchro Reader, but he took full responsibility for its commercial failure and urged us to "turn the misfortune into a blessing."

As it turned out, this expensive mistake produced invaluable assets. Ending the Syncro Reader left Canon with an entire factory and a lot of electronics engineers who had been employed for that product and suddenly had nothing to do. They went into another development program—and came up with calculator products, a continuing source of profit.

There was yet another merit. Canon, which previously had only camera dealers, for the first time with Syncro Reader established relationships with retailers of office machines. Preserving those links was very costly in the shortterm, but worth it later. On my recommendation, Canon's senior management authorized buying back from dealers all their inventories of Syncro Reader. This led to a very smooth entry into the office-machine market five years later when Canon introduced its calculators. The dealers very willingly welcomed our product line.

Personally, I gained two lasting benefits. At a young age, that aborted product exposed me to office-machine dealers—and in good style because I was able to repurchase inventories at the full price they had paid. One major office-machine dealer, called Moriichi, took a liking to me and treated me almost like a protégé, writing letters of introduction to most major dealers of office machines and products in Japan. Through him, I was able to establish successful relationships with virtually all the major office-machine dealers throughout the country.

I also gained an entry visa into Canon's planning of other new businesses. In the days of Syncro Reader, product development was primarily handled by technical people, and only a few top executives were involved. Today, a diverse group, including marketing people, participate in decisions about introducing new products.

Equally important are the insights I gained from the Syncro Reader experience. It was a typical failure caused by the lack of a proper scenario for the product. We paid a high price for learning that you must do careful product planning to build a business. A corollary is that you cannot work with an unsuccessful product very long; there has to be a cutoff time. But you must end things in a way so that you can always return to the scene.

10

My 105 Percent Solution to Layoffs: Make Selling a Science

The American recession of 1974 forced me, as president of Canon U.S.A., to lay off 50 U.S. employees—a terrible experience. As a result, I promised myself that no company I managed would ever again have a layoff. From that desire was born my 105 percent solution, based on my philosophy that selling is a science.

For me, the entrepreneurial spirit makes life enjoyable and fun. But many business people feel confronted with endless work in an intensely competitive society—and, thus, need a management standard that lifts their spirit. My approach is to build some comfort and reserve space into the basic structure of sales work. At the same time, I expect salesmen to attain 105 percent of their targets.

My theory sprang from the hard realities of the marketplace. On returning to Japan in 1977 to manage Canon's domestic sales, I noticed a pattern in our generally listless performance. Most sales and deliveries were concentrated at the end of each month. And about half the annual volume of business was shoved into the month of March, when the fiscal year ended. This practice, still followed by some camera manufacturers in Japan, is very costly: To move that much merchandise, you have to give extraordinary discounts and extended payment terms. The system also balloons the company's costs for warehouses and manpower, which move huge volumes of inventory during a few months but are underemployed most of the year. There was nothing good about this arrangement. I often heard horror stories in Japan about salesmen who hustled like mad at the end of the month to reach their quotas, but loafed around the rest of the month.

The difference between the American and the Japanese styles of doing business comes into play here, too. In the United States, it was much easier to carry out this plan because dealers there will often give you a three-month commitment, while in Japan they give orders month by month. I do not know why this difference exists. In the United States, if you manage your three-month commitments well, then you can carry out a smooth-curve operation. But in Japan, you need to plan ahead and hedge.

Rather than having these peaks and valleys, I wanted steady sales throughout each month, forming a smooth curve on a graph. This activity, however, is conducted among humans, so some ups and downs are inevitable. To compensate for that, I came up with a kind of back-order system. An ordinary back order is placed by a customer for specific months in the future. My kind is different: A sale that has taken place in, say, April is reported in May.

Why bother? This supports my idea that a salesman performs best after tasting success. Similarly, if the salesman has some back orders to start the month (and we count them as sales), he feels comfortable to continue selling. Rather than lumping the sales made toward the end of the month, we save them until the following month to make the salesman feel comfortable in starting a new month.

My insistence on achieving 105 percent of the budgeted sales target is based on the same thinking. Human beings are funny animals. Most people will create a plan and get a net result of 96 percent to 98 percent—and think that is good enough. By setting a 105 percent plan though, there is no reason why anyone would go under 100 percent. Anyone who falls below 100 percent, in fact, might not be around for long.

The 105 percent solution provides surprisingly consistent results. My graph is a model for what I consider to be a scientific approach to sales. In an ideal situation, sales continue on a straight line through the month. In reality, however, I continue to build sales until the 25th of the month, after which anything attained is carried over to the following month. That portion realized between the 25th and the end of the month is billed at the beginning of the following month—so the sales graph rises rapidly at the start of the month. By the tenth of the month, sales are already coming in at a comfortable level. Our people will continue to sell normally between the 10th and the 20th of the month.

The actual sales pattern has twin peaks. Figure 1 illustrates this. Most Japanese companies have their purchasing and billing cycles on the 20th of each month.

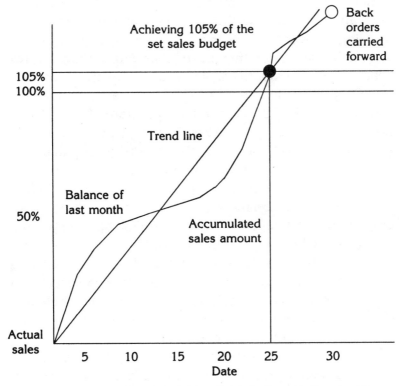

Figure 1. Basic Sales Model by "Sales Is Science Standard."

Consequently, the salesman who has enjoyed comfortable results during this period starts to work really hard on the 20th because he has to close for the month. Without the twin-peak approach, the salesman will work like hell at the end of the month to meet his quota and start the new month completely tired.

By carrying over those back orders, the salesmen have a comfort zone to do their work and are not apt to give excessive discounts. They are very strong-willed, aggressive, and not afraid of losing an order. Furthermore, they have plenty of time for sales calls. The salesmen from other companies tend to make a far greater number of visits to dealers toward the end of the month to meet their quotas. But Canon salespeople start at the beginning of the month, focusing on new products that you do not discount. Toward the end of the month, they push all products. Climbing two peaks during the month usually results in greater total sales.

Only twice in the past 15 years have we failed to accomplish the 105 percent sales program. The first time was in 1986, when the value of the yen just shot up against the dollar, and all of our back orders were quickly depleted. We ended up with 98 percent of the plan, resulting in a profit reduction of 35 percent compared with the year before. Other companies had far worse results, though. In 1992, we also could not attain the 105 percent goal; but we stayed in the black while many competitors were losing money.

Once the twin-peak pattern and 105 percent plan are lost, there is no longer a comfort zone—and people will work hard just meeting the quota. Marketing is not fun at all then. Moreover, salesmen no longer have the leeway to take a forward leap and to think aggressively.

This method is more than merely a psychological game. Attaining 100 percent of the sales target can cover expenses and usually about 3 percent profit. A sales organization has many fixed expenses—personnel, office space, and advertising—that cannot be canceled on short notice. Once sales fall under 100 percent, profits are immediately affected. Achieving 105 percent of the target yields a handsome profit and makes a company highly resistant to temporary fluctuations of the economy.

We veer to the conservative side in forming the sales budget, of course. But we must have a precise forecast of work so that the 105 percent goal can be achieved. I will accept relatively low targets under two conditions. The first condition is that the target must be within reason, at least keeping pace with the economy's growth rate and not falling below the performance of the previous year. The second condition is that the operational budget for each salesman is based on the 100 percent performance level. Thus, the lower the given sales budget, the lower the operational expenses. But I still expect 105 percent performance.

A comfortable rhythm of sales can be built up with a twin-peak operation. We sweat a little at the beginning of the month to build some savings, then take a breath in the middle of the month, and finally climb the second peak. That is how I have kept my company growing at an average rate of 15 percent annually for the past 15 years.

11

Why a Chief Executive Should Review Expense Accounts

Though my company has over 9,000 employees, I regularly look over the expense accounts of many senior managers and some of our younger people. My purpose is not to pinch a few yen, but to gain valuable information.

I learned this technique from Dr. Takeshi Mitarai, our late chairman, who insisted on getting big stacks of expense reports every day. He looked at not only high-ticket items, but also those for a few thousand yen. I wondered about this for a long time I could not stand my puzzlement any longer, and finally asked him why he looked at all those reports. His answer really impressed me. He was not looking at the numbers, but diagonally across the expense reports to see what kind of activities the employees were conducting—at what level, with whom, in what district. And he could sense from those reports a lot about the business on which employees were working—people with whom they were associating and the kinds of negotiations they were conducting.

Consequently, I use expense reports as a kind of management information system. In good times, employees get a little frivolous and the expense reports stack up really high. In recessions, when we have some belt-tightening, the stack gets thin. By looking at each report, I can readily identify with whom our managers are dealing, what they are discussing, what level of business talks are taking place. Often this alerts me to how some large potential deals are shaping up.

Many Japanese companies lately have been tightening their belts because of sluggish sales. Some companies have even cut salaries of senior executives, postponed pay increases for others, and laid off workers. Canon has not resorted to such moves, though. First, during slow periods, a company naturally watches expenses more closely, but cannot attack all costs with a meat axe. Canon Sales, for example, makes advertising commitments for an entire season on popular television programs in Japan. If that were cancelled, it would be very difficult to get back on. Therefore, the best approach is to cut other TV spot commercials.

Secondly, entertainment expenses are reduced, and, thirdly, special sales events can be modified to cut costs. For instance, a dealer's meeting in good times might be held in the luxurious Imperial Hotel in Tokyo, but in rough times, we look for a more economical auditorium near our offices. Travel expenses are difficult to conserve, but I ask people to do their best.

Overtime pay is conserved as much as possible. Of course, whatever overtime people do on their own, voluntarily and without pay, is another matter. At factories, the work load automatically goes down during a recession, so that is a self-adjusting feature. In slow periods, we reduce purchases of equipment and materials—and also ask for better prices from suppliers.

Cutting compensation to employees, however, comes only as a last resort. Any company that has to make pay cuts and curb compensation is really having a hard time. The only time I have ever seen that happen in our group was in 1986, when both Canon Inc. and Canon Sales had to institute pay cuts for officers. Having the company's best-paid executives make a sacrifice sets a good example for everyone else.

12

How To Find Managers Who Are Leaders

*O*n the Old Testament, I came across a description of a man as a leader of either 10, 100, or 1,000. I was impressed with that idea.

If a person who is best at managing 10 people is given the task of leading 100 people, the team will succumb to failure. It is crucial to determine whether a person is a leader of 10, 100, or 1,000. Success in any company is greatly determined by how well the top management can identify leaders of 10, 100, or 1,000 people.

In my 38 years with the Canon Group, I have served as a company president for a total of 22 years, and, before that, all my time in the company had been spent dedicated to personnel, in one way or another. My experiences as personnel manager of the Canon Group for eight years before going to America proved especially valuable. I had the advantage of knowing the people inside the Canon Group. That enabled me to select those best suited for working with me at Canon U.S.A. Initially, I was not concerned about their English-speaking ability, but looked for people with specific areas of expertise, such as finance or sales of cameras and other product lines. I felt their experience provided a reasonable chance for success. After all, in those days, the difference in the English-speaking ability of those well-qualified in a particular area was not that much greater than anyone else in the company. I feel the success rate is determined by a well-balanced combination of technical specialists and generalists.

In 22 years, of course, I have made some misjudgments. But as soon as one finds that a man is not a 100-person manager, one must take quick action to bring him back to a position of overseeing 10 people. This is particularly important in judging who's most suitable to be a 1,000-person manager.

I have been fortunate enough to have the right person

to help me at the right time—which I call a relationship in fate. In other words, certain people seem to be linked to you by fate. An example of a fated relationship is Seymour Liebman, who is now treasurer and vice-president of Canon U.S.A. A few years after I became president of that company, we took over our products from American distributors and handled their sales. Liebman, who was a certified public accountant at Peat Marwick, came on my request to join Canon U.S.A. For us to get a young hotshot CPA as an employee was more than we could hope for back then, when Canon was a fairly minor company in America. Without his presence at that time, the company would never have done so well. He joined when Canon's American operation had annual revenues of perhaps $100 million; today annual sales are over $4 billion.

The Canon Group is almost unique, at least in Japan, in its tradition of allowing capable people from other companies to join us in the midstream of their careers. I was fortunate in being able to hire such people—getting energy transfusions to reinvigorate our staff. Canon has many people who have transferred from Olivetti, IBM, or elsewhere. And uniquely, perhaps, for a Japanese company, there is not much friction inside Canon between those who joined immediately after graduation from university and those midstream people who joined later in their careers.

I do not pay much attention to where people come from. Perhaps this comes from my experience at the age of five of being moved from one relative to another, which helped me to value many associations with people at all levels of society. I never resist bringing in the necessary people from whatever source.

Part of my life's philosophy is to put people into better, higher, and more challenging positions. I try to expand the scope of their work and their spheres of influence. Almost everyone sees that when a person does well on my team, he gets promoted eventually. So others in our company look forward to promotion, too. It is very important to me to improve everyone's position and income, to promote able people into better positions. This is what attracts able people to our company. The moment I stop such efforts, people will stop coming to me.

I always provide an environment in which good managers can come to me for shelter and support. There is a Japanese phrase about taking off your woven straw sandals, which means your journey is over and you have found a place that provides food and shelter. I try to offer an environment in which the weak can look for shelter. A good manager must give people that feeling.

One of the beliefs I have had since childhood is that when someone comes to you for help, giving them money is only a temporary solution. Providing employment is more likely to give them permanent relief; this leads to a long-term relationship and improves the chances of success. This is a common feeling anywhere in the world: Giving cash is a short-term solution, but employment is a more permanent solution. That is what the economic process is all about.

As time progresses and people get to know that my company has activities that create more employment, they come to me. As long as I live, I want to continue to create ways to provide more and better employment.

In Japan, I have had to terminate employment of a few people, solely for two reasons: sexual harassment and improprieties with company funds. Even then, firing an employee is very undesirable. Another undesirable task is demotion. This takes place when senior executives misjudged whether someone is a 10-man manager or a 100-man manager. Everyone has ego and pride, but few realize that they are only a 10-man manager. Unless you rigorously enforce this principle of having the right managers in the right jobs, a company cannot function well.

It is very difficult to continue creating more jobs. Canon Sales has an attrition rate of only 4 percent a year. In a weak economy—like Japan has experienced recently—I do not want to lay off anyone. Instead, I rely on attrition, which should trim about 700 people in two years. This is probably the only approach necessary in a company like Canon.

The role of our many smaller affiliated companies is extremely important. In the past few years, Canon Sales has hired 1,000 people a year, and they need promotion opportunities. So growth of smaller companies will create the demand for more managers—and positions for many of our people.

Job creation probably sounds like the goal of U.S. President Bill Clinton, and, in a way, our goals are the same. He, of course, is president of the United States of America, and I am only president of one company in Japan. But our basic objectives are the same—creating meaningful employment for our constituents.

Though it is not my primary objective to be number one or number two in our industry or only to optimize profits, those are necessary steps. Unless a company attains a certain status in its industry and earns profits, job opportunities cannot be created. Those goals are embedded in my objective. You must have profits and status to do what I am trying to do.

Giving top priority to creating meaningful jobs can be done only if a chief executive is reasonably comfortable about the length of his tenure. If that is only going to last four to six years, how can one think of cultivating seedling companies? It often takes 10 years to nurture a new venture into success or turn around an acquisition.

American business practices, which stress short-term results, often destroy the chances of planting seeds of new business. But there are some benefits of the American way. Look at John Sculley at Apple and other Americans who became chief executives in their early fifties or younger. In theory, they should have a better chance of carrying out a long-term plan because they start younger than their Japanese counterparts. In Japan, the average chief executive starts in his late fifties to early sixties, which is too late. We never heard of Japanese CEOs in their early fifties until recently. I was 52 when Canon Sales was listed on the first section of the Tokyo Stock Exchange—but I have always done things a bit differently from others in Japan.

Once, colleagues at Nippon Telephone & Telegraph asked me, "What is the real job of a company president?" It boils down to just two main things. First, he is the man who goes around collecting and expanding opportunities to spur the company's growth. Second, he must be absolutely certain that when payday comes, he can cover the payroll with cash in the bank.

It is not easy finding new business, of course. Unless one keeps feeding and fostering small companies within the Canon group, a recession can be very ruinous. The job of the president is to feed and seed for the future. Finding new opportunities obviously is not the job of the president alone, but he does it by mobilizing a capable staff.

If there is not enough new business coming along, it is risky to hire too many people because most of them aspire to becoming managers. Deprived of that chance, they can be lured away to other companies after they are trained.

117

I know that others say that the main job of a chief executive is to assure that the company is a leader in its industry or that profits are maximized. As simple as my goals may sound, the fact that a company has money to cover the payroll means that it is financially strong, does not have to lay off people, and, therefore, is a healthy company.

13

How To Wake Up a Sleeping Company

*A*s president of Canon U.S.A. in the 1970s, I was in the midst of building a nationwide network for direct sales of office equipment to consumers, but suddenly was compelled to return to Japan. President Takeo Maeda, who headed both manufacturing and sales in Japan for the Canon Group, passed away. In January 1977, I had to become president of Canon Sales—which was a sleeping company. Its initial work force was about 1,500. Staff members who were moved from the parent company to my new operation were anxious and dissatisfied. To reassure them, I set as a major goal to build an excellent company and obtain an independent listing on the Tokyo stock exchange. In effect, I had to carry out in Japan my plans for creating a U.S. sales network.

Canon Sales Co., despite its grand name, had absolutely no one selling office equipment directly to consumers. That meant that we had no means of doing hands-on market research or of supporting our dealers. Consequently, our market share for plain-paper copying machines was stuck at 10 percent. Toward the end of 1977, I was fully determined to mount a protracted struggle to triple our market share, a mind-boggling goal at the time.

My American experience provided an inspiration. In the United States, I gained a hard-won lesson that it is not viable to develop salesmen both for direct sales and for wholesale business in the same location. So back in Japan, I made up my mind to start a new experiment—creating an organization to sell office equipment directly to consumers. This enterprise, called Canon Eiken, would earn its own way and try out new ways of marketing.

It is people, of course, who make a company. Hideo Tani, an executive vice-president, seemed just the right man to lead the new sales organization—but he resisted the job. Tani, a former captain in the old Japanese army, spent four years in Siberia. Upon his return to Japan, he founded an office-equipment sales firm and later merged it with our company. Ten years my senior, Tani is among the many dogmatic people in our company.

In the beginning of December 1977, I invited Tani into my office to discuss the idea of Canon Eiken. I wanted him to be its vice president and director of sales. I vividly remember the response of Tani, who was then 55 years old.

He said, "I had a plan similar to yours, President Takikawa, and presented it to your predecessor several years ago, but it was turned down. The copying-machine industry now (about 1977) is dominated 70 percent to 80 percent (in terms of market share) by Xerox and Ricoh Co. In other words, the PPC [plain-paper copier] war is already over. And for us to try to establish a new company called Canon Eiken for capturing a 30 percent market share is like Japan thinking about resuming fighting after accepting the Potsdam Declaration [which required unconditional surrender for ending World War II]. It is a very reckless act."

For nearly one month, I kept on trying to persuade Tani, who kept saying, "You cannot resume fighting after accepting the Potsdam Declaration." As the end of the year was fast approaching, I finally pleaded that it was not manly of him to resist my pleas for his help. He retorted, "Well, even a man cannot fight after accepting the Potsdam Declaration."

Finally, I told him I would take the job myself, but later I heard that he saw no other choice but to resign from our company—which disturbed me even more than his unyielding refusals. That night, while drinking my sake in a down-and-out spirit, I thought of going to the one person who was most persuasive, Dr. Takeshi Mitarai, already in his mid-seventies and not active in operations but still the leader of the Canon Group.

Next morning, I went to the head office of Canon Inc. and luckily found that Dr. Mitarai was at the company that day. I told him about my month-long series of discussions with Tani and the frustrating results. Dr. Mitarai said, "Mr. Takikawa, tell Mr. Tani that someone in his fifties and sixties is a young kid. He should be able to understand what I am saying when he hears this."

I hurried back to my office and related to Mr. Tani, "The old man told me to tell you that a man in his fifties or sixties is still just a kid with a runny nose." This remark penetrated me deeply as well. I, too, was still young and immature. I had been trying to convince Tani simply with logic alone. What really persuaded Tani was that I had firmly set my heart on his support, as evidenced by my seeking advice from Dr. Mitarai. Tani finally accepted the assignment, beginning a genuinely entrepreneurial sales organization.

From the start, all our new employees initially worked a few years at Canon Eiken, selling directly to end-users of Canon products. Besides serving as a training institute, this sales organization had to earn its way and would experiment with new kinds of sales techniques. We had high hopes, but we began slowly in February 1978 with only 14 salesmen in the Tokyo metropolitan area. I had more than a few complaints from sales managers in our own company who did wholesaling to dealers. The Canon managers resented losing good people to this direct sales organization—which they called "the royal domain of the president."

Many of our dealers worried that we were going to compete with them, so I patiently went around explaining why we needed to sell to consumers. With a market share of just 10 percent, it is difficult to cut costs of Canon copiers—and help dealers win in price competition with competitors. Moreover, Canon Eiken—once it gained experience in selling—could train personnel of our dealers. Eventually, the dealers realized we were acting to strengthen their sales position. And, gradually, our new sales organization gained strength and ability.

I will never forget one training session that Canon Eiken held for managers and supervisors. I decided to attend the third and final day of the program to hear its conclusion. When I looked into the room, papers listing nearly innumerable problems were posted on all the walls. Every point had some validity and sounded reasonable, but there was not even one solution or new idea proposed to deal with these problems. Put another way, I could not detect any entrepreneurial spirit at all. So my temper just exploded. I was only about 46 years old, full of vigor, very impatient.

In my fury, I said, "What are managers and supervisors? What are your roles? I don't remember asking you merely to manage or supervise. You're supposed to be active managers, real playing managers who get out and sell. Unless you set an example, your subordinates will not make a move. And there are only two things that playing managers can do. One is to set a good example, and the other is to motivate your group. If the section chief sets the example by selling the most, then his subordinates will sell as well. However, as a rule, because shopping is enjoyable and sales activity is severe, you motivate people by figuring out how to lead everyone, how to push out bright vision, and how to reflect and think of conversation topics for salesmen. That would be an excellent way of motivating your people.

"Instead, you have spent two whole days just listing problems, but you have not come up with even one solution, one new suggestion, or an interesting way of motivating people. Practical wisdom does not come out unless you suffer through and forge experiences with your people. For listing problems, you don't need any brains. I think that you should end this useless discussion meeting right away!"

The 15 or so supervisors were stunned but got the point. I thought to myself that perhaps I came off too strong and said too much. Still, if this first fruit of entrepreneurship by our company got afflicted with a big-business disease, then our hopes and dreams would come to naught. So I persisted in pushing these ideas—hard. And within 12 years, Canon Eiken achieved all of its goals splendidly.

My steak party helped, too. Canon Eiken's sales force was constantly under pressure and confronted rivals that had more personnel. I decided to invite those salesmen who gained the most copier orders to a special dinner each month. At various times, we ate broiled eels, Chinese food, or tiger's testicles (because it supposedly gave us pep). I exchanged dreams with young salesmen, hoping to build up their confidence. Gradually, as sales grew, the number of salesmen invited to the monthly dinners increased. And, eventually, the favorite meal was a steak weighing over one pound—which made the gathering come to be known as the "Inner Circle Steak Party" group, that is, a steak-dinner-party group within the company family.

Today, the name of this dinner has been changed to "Inner Outstanding Sales Dinner Group." It is held twice a year in Tokyo and Osaka for several hundred people—a mark of success for our salespeople. There are so many, in fact, that I spend those evenings just shaking hands and talking to everybody.

My company is really awake now. In just 15 years, we have profitably increased sales tenfold to more than $4 billion annually. We are listed on the Tokyo Stock Exchange. And I am still prodding people to think like entrepreneurs and avoid the bureaucratic disease that afflicts many big companies.

14

Japan Needs Its Own Style for Mergers and Acquisitions

usinesspeople should forget about attempting American-style mergers and acquisitions in Japan. To me, an enterprise is not just a piece of merchandise. It is a place where people work, a foundation for their lives. Having taken over a number of Japanese companies myself and merged them with Canon Sales Co., I believe this has to be done in a distinctively Japanese style.

When someone takes over a corporation in America, the first goal is to make the acquisition profitable. In Japan, while profit is certainly the objective, one also must carefully respect the personal feelings of people working in the acquired company. This is a very touchy matter for Japanese. We even have a special name for a company that buys out another firm: *shinchugun*, the term used for American soldiers who occupied Japan after World War II. If employees of an acquired company get that feeling, then it is extremely difficult to make a merger work well.

By its nature, a takeover is an inhuman procedure. Knowing that has made me all the more sensitive to the emotions and the pecking order of the people involved. None of my acquisitions, of course, have been hostile. I have assumed responsibility for another company only after being invited by a management that has run into serious difficulties. Rather than acting like a conqueror, I concentrate on providing capital and support so that the company's own managers and employees can strengthen that company.

Even my Japanese-style acquisitions are never easy work, though. After leading several successful turnarounds of acquired companies, I found people around me telling various legendary tales about how we overcame big obstacles. My men become convinced that once the boss says something, he will surely succeed. They never even think of failure. On the contrary, I always secretly worry about how things will go. Then as the game advances, morale soars—including mine.

Nothing excites an entrepreneur more than a new opportunity. In assuming the presidency of Canon Sales Co. in 1977, my big goal was to attain a dominant position in Japan for Canon copying machines—which then had only a 10 percent market share. My first struggle was to expand our rather limited sales force. Toward the end of 1979, a big present dropped from heaven, a present that demanded a great deal of study if I were to be capable of using it. Copyer Co., which was listed on the Tokyo stock exchange and had a national sales force, was drowning in red ink. I was asked to rebuild that company by its president Yukio Oya. He came to see me and expressed concern about meeting his social responsibilities to employees and their families even though he was no longer able to keep the company going. President Oya wanted to resign but hoped to save the company by handing it over to us. Here was a chief executive willing to sacrifice himself so that his company could survive. He immediately earned my full respect.

At that time, Copyer Co. already had a history of 60 years but had failed to ride the crest of technological innovation. The company made diazo-type copiers that use photosensitive paper, a product that declined with the growing popularity of plain-paper copiers (known as PPC in the business). As the 1970s came to a close, Copyer Co. made valiant efforts to develop a PPC and tried to sell machines made by others. But the company ended up with large losses and could not continue without new financing. That troubled company, however, had an asset that very much appealed to me—a network of 50 direct-sales subsidiaries, one in each prefecture, and 200 dealers throughout Japan. Those sales channels could greatly strengthen Canon and help attain my goal, a 30 percent share of the Japanese copier market.

Consequently, I presented to President Oya my confidential plan for turning Copyer Co. around. To make things as smooth as possible, I would become president of Copyer Sales Company. This is unusual in Japan, where, ordinarily, another executive is sent to head an acquisition. Though we would take over, I decided that Copyer should be restructured by its own hands. We would assist in every possible way, but not take over its management. Copyer, however, would have to be divided—with its manufacturing facilities placed under Canon Inc. (my parent company) and the sales components coming under my wing.

President Oya himself agreed to all this on the spot, and we began quietly working out the details with our subordinates—but made no announcement. This kind of deal is hard to keep secret, though. Within a few weeks, the leading Japanese business newspaper, *Nihon Keizai Shimbun,* broke the story before the acquisition had been explained to the trade union at Copyer Co. This caused a lot of chaos at the company for a while, but I finally decided to meet with the union leaders myself. This was highly unusual because the merger had not yet taken place, but I wanted to understand the worries and anxieties of Copyer's employees. The meeting turned out to be a good opportunity to reassure them.

I felt that this acquisition was a task entrusted to me by heaven and that I had to make it a success. So I made up my mind to use all the best means that I could think of. For entrepreneurs, whether starting a new company or rebuilding one, half the battle is winning the trust of the employees.

After the takeover, there was still much uneasiness, so I decided to go around the country and meet all the 1,200 employees. During my six years as president of Canon Copyer, I spent the equivalent of two years visiting all the facilities, talking to just about every individual in the organization and trying to convince them that I was not a conqueror or *shinchugun*, but rather one who just wanted to make the company successful. In meetings at noodle shops and while drinking sake together, I insisted that no one stand on ceremony or treat me like a big shot. I explained my belief that a company consists mainly of its employees—and asked them to trust me. Gradually, my ideas came to be accepted and were put into effect. The acquisition was reborn as Canon Copyer Sales Co., a name change that was requested by its employees.

Our turnaround strategy boiled down to a few basic themes. To reduce overhead expenses, most employees (including senior managers) had to become salesmen and call on customers. We had to stick to a policy of securing at least 30 percent gross profits, never discounting our prices. We needed to be courageous in abolishing all bad accounts receivable and defective inventory so that our figures showed the true state of the company. And, of course, everyone had to learn my basic principle of achieving 105 percent of sales targets.

In the summer of 1980, young employees of Canon Eiken, my premier sales organization, took officers and supervisors of Copyer on unannounced, door-to-door calls on customers. I wanted the managers to learn how to sell products directly to our end-users, which Copier Co. people had never done before. They knew, at least in theory, that a salesperson must make 30 sales calls a day. But they really understood it only after going out and doing it themselves in the summer heat. And doing it together with Canon Eiken salesmen showed them that we were not occupying

Copyer Co. Eventually, we retrained the entire sales force to sell Canon copying machines the Canon way.

Watching that company grow healthy really was a great feeling. By 1982, Copyer Sales was already operating in the black. Several years later, the company went public as an over-the-counter stock in Japan. Its sales last year totaled some $500 million, and we are aiming for $1 billion by the year 2000.

Though I did not realize it, an investment banker was watching my efforts—which led to another big acquisition. In June 1985, managers of the merger-and-acquisitions division of Yamaichi Securities suggested a tie-up with Nippon Typewriter Co., known as NTC. It was in trouble.

This distinguished maker of Japanese-language type-writers, which had been in business for more than 70 years, had built a near monopoly by supplying its machines to government agencies and schools. It had been one of the major office equipment companies, a model business. No corporation, however, can prosper basically unchanged for more than 30 years. In all fields, technological innovations produce new products; but yesterday's new products become obsolete tomorrow. By the 1980s, cheaper word-processing machines had taken over most of the Japanese typewriter market. In 1985, NTC sold off some of its assets but still lost money. As the physicist Stephen Hawking says in his book *A Brief History of Time*, even the black hole of the great universe undergoes changes; it is born and then dies. Perhaps this is the law of the great universe.

In June 1985, at my first meeting with President Shigeo Sakurai of NTC, he appeared to be searching for a partner to help revive his company's business. Having heard about its situation from Yamaichi Securities, I told him, "Your sales network appeals to us, and the simplest thing would be just to take over your company. Instead, I prefer that you continue running the company, and we'll be happy to provide merchandise that is easier to sell."

President Sakurai, who was almost 65 years old, had other ideas. Uncertain that he could turn around the company, he wanted to hand its management to me. I accepted.

Perhaps Mr. Sakurai had heard about the methods that we used to rebuild Copyer Co., but I was still quite moved by his attitude, especially his sense of obligation to his employees. We trusted each other from the start.

Within a week or so, Sakurai came back and, to my surprise, said, "I won consent from all directors. Here's the power of attorney, so please buy up all our shares." We had met only once before this. Besides, only about 10 percent of his company's shares were available on the market—which we purchased. His offer would have been understandable if we had over 51 percent ownership, but with a mere 10 percent interest and without any condition, he offered the resignations of all directors from the president down and asked me to take over everything.

This put me under great pressure to prove worthy of his trust. Rather than feeling that I had bought a company, I felt a great obligation to improve its condition and take a load off the minds of its employees. On the other hand, if many conditions are attached to a deal, one becomes weary before the real work begins.

For nearly a month, I went around, unobtrusively, to the headquarters of NTC, its plants, and major sales offices, while one of my executives came to grips with the details of the company's financial condition. The very next month, we signed an official agreement. President Sakurai and four directors who were at the age of 65 or older resigned voluntarily. They seemed to be relieved at the opportunity to hand over responsibility to younger people and make a clean withdrawal.

Everything moved very fast with NTC. In September 1985, we started rebuilding the company, despite a sudden shift in the economic climate. International trade frictions had unexpectedly created a stronger Japanese yen, slowing down the economy. As a result, Canon Inc. decided against investing in this troubled typewriter company, so my Canon Sales Co. had to act alone. And we decided not to divide the manufacturing and sales components of NTC. I wound up being responsible for reviving the entire acquisition.

Rebuilding the sales division proceeded quickly, primarily because NTC had many experienced salespeople. Once again, Canon's sales organization trained managers and supervisors at NTC by making the rounds of customers—and selling Canon products. NTC, of course, adopted my management standards for carrying out the principle that selling is a science. I rallied everyone around a slogan: "Let us build a 100 billion yen company with high efficiency and high pay." That sales goal—equivalent to $800 million—was nearly 10 times the highest volume that NTC had ever achieved, but the company is already halfway toward attaining the ambitious target. It has been operating in the black since 1987 and wiped out all the accumulated losses by the first half of 1990.

Again, I discovered how enjoyable is the life of an entrepreneur. The former typewriter company has become an important channel for computers as well as copiers and other office equipment. There were hardly any discordant notes between the dealers of NTC, on one hand, and the other Canon dealers. They have all become accustomed to inevitable shakeups in an industry where technology changes fast.

In contrast, reshaping the production at Nippon Type-writer was really difficult at the beginning. Production of Japanese-language typewriters had dropped drastically, its work force had been sharply cut, and the manufacturing equipment was obsolete. We scurried around for production contracts to keep the factories going. But manufacturers that could give us work were struggling with the effects of the high yen, which pressured big exporters into moving production overseas. Consequently, we had a tough time getting manufacturing contracts from Canon.

I went around visiting my old colleagues in all the companies in the Canon Group, bowing my balding head. Half in despair, NTC developed an electronic blackboard so that it would have something to make, but its sales did not go well. We were saved in 1988, when the Japanese economy began to recover and went into a really long upswing. A year later, we decided to build the most advanced plating and coating plant for making components of Canon products.

What saved the day—and paid for the new plant—was a latent asset of this old Japanese typewriter company. It had some valuable land that was not being used. I discovered that an investment group was making speculative purchases of NTC stock in hopes of gaining control of the company's land in Tokyo. To quash that speculative play, I increased our company's equity in NTC from about 20 percent to about 50 percent. Then I figured that selling the company's idle land in Tokyo would pay for building its new plant. In short, NTC could have the most advanced production technology without incurring any debt. To an entrepreneur, this plant is like a beautiful poem or painting—but one that will play a creative role into the twenty-first century.

All my acquisitions, including several software firms, were troubled companies that we turned around by using a few basic principles. Most of all, I invest myself in acquisitions. I assume the presidency of important subsidiaries until they get strong enough to show a profit because I want all our employees to assist that acquisition. The debts of a subsidiary are treated as our own. Canon Sales Co., however, never indulges in the common Japanese practice of off-loading to a subsidiary older personnel we do not want.

When one takes over a company in Japan, one also acquires a moral obligation. By operating with that attitude, I have gained enormous rewards—both material and spiritual.

15

Why a Company Needs Lively Young People

I like working with young people who are not too bureaucratic, but this is really nothing new to our country.

The people in the Meiji Restoration era (1868–1912) deserve the credit for establishing those notable organizations called corporations. Young Japanese pioneers, who were in their thirties or early forties, went to the West on their own, established businesses, and returned to Japan to create great enterprises. Their remarkable efforts helped our country to break away from two centuries of self-imposed isolation from the world—and to quickly modernize. The splendid entrepreneurial spirit of the Meiji Restoration reverted back to more bureaucratic tendencies after Japan entered the Showa period, a change that is truly regrettable. I think that authentic things are born out of the practice of having every one of the 100 million Japanese become critics. Looking at those people in the Meiji era, perhaps, makes those in the Showa era that followed appear a little lethargic.

Even now, however, when companies are small, people are very dynamic and energetic—showing entrepreneurial qualities like those in the Meiji era. Once companies start growing, though, the bureaucratic element usually slows them down.

Therefore, I feel that it is my duty to really look for young, ambitious, capable, energetic people in their thirties and early forties. I put them on track in our corporation; on their own, they expand the potential of the company.

What helps Canon a lot is a policy that I helped develop as personnel manager: Promotion of our people does not depend mainly on seniority, as it does in many traditional Japanese companies; Canon employees rise largely on ability and performance.

The most promising people get on a fast track early in their careers at Canon. Some 15 years ago, Tohru Kaneko caught my eye as a capable sales manager at the age of 35. He was trusted both by those who were above him and by those serving under him. Today, he is a managing director who leads over 2,000 staff members of the System Eiken division of our company. Kaneko's background and experience are not what you usually find in a large corporation. He became a civil servant after graduating from college, but soon resigned and became a seaman on an American merchant ship, mainly to study and see first-hand (at some risk to himself) the Vietnam war and the world at large. After this adventure, he joined our company and developed into a superb salesman. Kaneko, a samurai with a fourth-degree black belt in judo, is living his life freely as his spirit commands him.

American company presidents are younger than their Japanese counterparts—a practice Japan probably should copy in order to compete. In the United States, not only business managers but even politicians tend to be younger. In Japan, I am beginning to see more and more people consider making use of younger people who are capable of assuming heavier responsibilities. Still, the Japanese have an ailment: While they think that way, they fall short when it comes to executing the idea of giving young people greater responsibility. This gets back to the custom of promotion by tenure rather than performance. If the promotion system is just let alone, it reverts back to tenure.

If an organization is allowed to just go along without any agitation, everyone becomes good buddies and they all grow old together. That is why I need to pick some younger people to play more responsible roles. Simultaneously, I feel the need for energy transfusions—bringing in people from outside to give spark and life in ways that are different from those realized by promoting from within the company. The best outsiders will shake up other managers, who may get fed up, but ultimately will gather new energy to compete. *Young* people often do this best, though.

16

My Big Future Hope: The Japanese-Cosmopolitan

Once I had built Canon U.S.A. into a formidable company, some American friends suggested that I should consider becoming a U.S. citizen. I was flattered by the suggestion and began thinking about the world in different terms.

Americans believe that the United States was created by people and races who came from throughout the world in search of freedom, peace, and prosperity. To them, being an American means being a member of the world's leading group of pioneers. Naturally, they feel a great deal of pride about this. This attitude underpins the view that the United States has a duty to defend freedom and peace in the world, a duty entrusted to the country by God Himself.

I could acquire American citizenship and live as a Japanese-American, which is certainly one way of living. For me, however, the idea of leaving the beautiful islands of Japan, the history of our people that is embedded in me, plus hot miso soup and warm steamed rice, hot tofu [bean curd], and warm sake would be unthinkable.

Still, I kept wondering if there was any way to be both a free global person and remain a Japanese belonging to the home country of Japan (of which I am totally a part). I kept thinking about this with all my energy. As a result of exhaustively using my limited brains on this question, I recalled how Americans were calling one another "Japanese-Americans," "Italian-Americans," and so on. So there should be ways of living and of being what may be called "Japanese-Cosmopolitan," "British-Cosmopolitan," or "Chinese-Cosmopolitan," and so on.

Rather than becoming a Japanese-American, I decided to be a Japanese-Cosmopolitan instead. When I said this to American friends, they laughed and understood.

To begin with, national boundaries mean very little these days in the way people live and in the economy of humankind. The idea of a national boundary, in fact, is something that human beings invented only several thousand years ago, and it is an artificial, provisional barrier at best. We are now living in a period when people can even dream about the United States of the World in the twenty-first century.

I believe that Japanese-Cosmopolitans will be working for the coexistence and symbiosis of the world's humanity as members of the United States of the World, and, in the process, they will help inform other people of the world about the history and culture of Japan. Admittedly, it will take perhaps another 50 years before we enter the era of the Japanese-Cosmopolitan.

A person cannot become a Japanese-Cosmopolitan just with "Yamato spirit" alone—that is, the spirit of Japanese people. Unless a Japanese has that spirit, however, he or she is not qualified to become a Japanese-Cosmopolitan, I believe. While living in the United States, I began to study about Japan in a hurried way. The reason is that Americans asked me so many things about Japan that I could not answer satisfactorily. A well-educated Japanese college graduate should be able to explain the highlights of Japan's ancient history, tell about Shinto and Buddhism, and know something about the modern philosophy of Japan. One peculiar aspect of our society is that most Japanese, except for a few Christians, get married in the old Japanese Shinto ceremony; when they die, their funeral services are conducted in the Buddhist manner; and at Christmas time, Japanese people eat Christmas cake. This way of life, this mixture, is not at all strange to most Japanese.

In many ways, though, Japan *is* a very strange country. Living in an island nation that was long isolated from the world, the Japanese people generally are shy with foreigners—and isolated today by a language barrier.

Engineers and scientists are able to communicate in the common language of the world, such as mathematics and formulas in physics. I believe that Japan's education system should teach students in humanities and social sciences about Japan's correct history and culture in a solid way. Only then will Japanese-Cosmopolitans be born.

There are still Japanese who have concepts of two distinct groups of people—Japanese and *gaijin* (foreigners). But, come to think of it, there is no nationality called *foreigners*. Instead, a large number of nationalities live on this earth.

And when Japanese come to understand this reality, Japanese-Cosmopolitans will be born. A new breed, the Japanese-Cosmopolitan must make efforts to learn the histories, cultures, and religions of the world—and try to understand them.

In the United States, for example, the feelings of people about democracy are far more advanced than in Japan. It has been almost 50 years since the creation of democracy in Japan, and, yet, democracy is still immature in Japan. Though Japan has been changing for the good, so-called individualism has not advanced as well as in the United States. The concepts of freedom of speech, freedom of religion, and other basic rights are now fairly well understood in Japan—but not yet in practical terms of what these rights should mean for everyone.

Japanese business people are more apt to be cosmopolitan than are politicians. Inside Canon and Canon Sales, there are a lot of people who have lived in Europe or the United States—and tend to understand the term *Japanese-Cosmopolitan*. But others in the company who have only visited abroad without living there still do not understand.

When I started a program to import products, most people inside Canon acted very cool. They wanted to know why we were selling other companies' products. That was the situation seven or eight years ago. Now, it has completely changed. Since 1986, when Japan had big trouble with trade friction, even the prime minister said that Japanese people should buy foreign products. Nowadays, the Japanese Ministry of International Trade and Industry asks 50 major Japanese companies to strive for a better balance between imports and exports. And the Canon group has a kind of trade-improving committee that is trying to increase imports. In trade matters, everyone is learning to be a bit more cosmopolitan.

Having managed a U.S. company with employees of many races and nationalities, I believe that Cosmopolitans—including Japanese—should abide by a number of rules:

1. For Cosmopolitans, the world is one integrated market, and the national boundaries are like boundaries between provinces or states of a single country.
2. We will respect the history, cultures, and religions of one another's home country.
3. We must be fair to everyone.
4. *Freedom* means that we are free to do what we want to do as long as we do not harm others. This is provided in the Constitution of the United States and in the Declaration of Human Rights of the French Revolution.
5. Under democracy, everyone has equal rights, but everyone also has the duty to abide by what was decided by the majority.
6. English is becoming the common language of the world, and so, while it is not easy, we should make the effort to learn it.

17

What I Learned Working in the American Market

*C*racking the American market for Canon taught me many things that are useful in Japan. American companies, however, would do well to remember that not every technique "made in the USA" will work as well in Japan. Still, I have brought home to Japan many elements of the American approach to management and sales.

One of the most important things I acquired in America is a sharper notion about the duties of a company president. In 1976, just before coming back to Japan, I decided to advertise the Canon AE-1 camera on U.S. network television—a genuine breakthrough. Few Japanese consumer products had run commercials on American networks. Our ads produced a dramatic jump in sales of cameras that retailed for about $250.

But those TV commercials taught me something even more important than the value of advertising. Many on our staff advised using Dentsu or some other Japanese advertising agency. But I insisted that we do it in an all-American way. I approached six U.S. ad agencies, and five of their presidents showed up in my office. It seemed unbelievable. That is real marketing. In Japan, the president of an advertising agency would seldom show up in a customer's office. That is when I learned that the president has to be the number one salesperson.

Other things that I experienced in the United States made me fond of the American style of management—much of which I have adopted. One of the things that I particularly liked about the U.S. style is that whenever a meeting is held, everyone gives comments, presents his or her case, and discusses things— sometimes quietly, sometimes violently. At the end, however, the head of the meeting makes a decision and everyone abides by it. In Japan, hardly anyone gives his or her comments, but, *after* the president's decision, they will complain about it behind the scenes. The American way is superior in this respect. So I try to tell all the managers, especially during training programs, to express their own opinions, not just sit there. But I still see so many managers who come with a pencil and a notebook ready, but do not write anything—or say anything at all.

In the United States, another difference in management style shows up when a company is acquiring a computer system. Regardless of what a computer was used for, my Japanese managers insisted that the computer be purchased and installed—and from there they would start working little by little accomplishing all the objectives of the system. The American managers protested against that approach, saying that never would they acquire any computer system until it had all the capabilities they needed. This fundamental difference was never resolved, so I stepped in and endorsed the American approach. Since then, my Japanese managers who served in the United States have become firm believers in getting everything right the first time with a computer system.

Another facet of American management that I really appreciate is contained in the phrase "report to." In the United States, when someone is employed, they usually ask, "To whom am I reporting?" They always have that in mind. That is not so in Japan, where you are just employed by the company and do not think of "reporting to" someone. I would like that idea established in Japan.

When I returned to Japan, I would call various group heads and ask for details of plans or for the actual results against the plans. The group heads often did not know. They would call the section heads, who had all the numbers and details. So I would tell the group heads, "You do not have the right to report to me. I don't need your reporting relationship, but I can go to the section heads because they have the answers I want." After a series of encounters like that with group heads, they really got on top of the numbers.

Within a year, they began to anticipate the kind of information for which I would ask and to memorize those numbers before showing up in my office.

Eleven people on our board of twenty-one have returned from the United States, where they worked for me. Our board meetings are quite Americanized. A lot of people express their opinions, and quite a few issues are resolved right there and then, which is rarely done in Japan.

The Japanese system of making decisions through consensus has evolved in such a way that now it is very difficult to determine who actually made a decision other than the group. The consensus system of making decisions is not 100 percent bad, but it is certainly not a way to make speedy decisions. Consequently, I am 90 percent an American-style manager, using two-way communication and acting as a scenario writer.

I have discovered one good thing about consensus decisions: The average Japanese senior managers know about many things that they do not really need to know about. Since the managers do not usually express opinions, their depth of knowledge is only seen when something like a recession hits. Then they organize a team to break through problems. During an economic downturn, when the company is under pressure, the consensus system spurs team work—a real plus.

Japanese have succeeded quite well outside of Japan, even when they could not make up their own minds, certainly could not speak English, and did not fully understand other countries or the people of those countries. Japanese have gone abroad and done what they had to do. That is the result of both consensus decisions and sticking together in a group task, plus perhaps just perseverance.

But as Japanese business increasingly becomes more global, it is difficult to continue the current pace with consensus decision making. To respond to situations, we have to accept at least 70 percent of the American management practices.

On the other hand, Americans who come to Japan and try to conduct business need to know and understand consensus decision making. You often see what appears to be a virtual lord, the president of a Japanese company, sitting at the top, and his vassals are down below. But it is frequently the vassals who are really making the decisions, not the lord. And if you keep on dealing with just the lord, you will accomplish nothing.

Americans, in fact, need to understand other Japanese practices. In the United States once a contract is signed—of course, with lawyers involved—the two contracting companies are thoroughly bound by what they have signed and live up to it. In Japan, that is not necessarily so. The Japanese company might sign a contract, but it is lived up to only for so long as the situation is the same. When the situation changes, the consensus decision making starts. The figureheads of the two companies get together and talk about it, reinterpreting that agreement in a way that seems favorable to both of them. In essence, it might be totally different from the original contract. They adjust things. And if Americans do not understand that the Japanese do this and try to stick to a contract rigidly, they can lose more than they would gain from being flexible.

When I went to the United States, I found myself in a country where the contract is really honored. Regardless of benefits, both parties lived up to the terms of the contract. Therefore, I learned to be bound by agreements. But back in Japan, even though I have signed a contract, if the situation has changed, then the other party and I will mutually make adjustments that satisfy both parties.

In many ways, I must admit that selling is more difficult

in Japan than in the United States. If a good product is introduced in the American market, it can sell instantly. In Japan, however, even a good product must have a strong brand name, the dealer network, and strong sales channels. When I went to the United States in 1970, Canon was not a well-known brand. But when we started selling automatic electronic cameras like the AE-1 and new copiers, our sales went up like a skyrocket. In short, the American market is much more dynamic than that of Japan.

The size of success in the United States will be bigger if the same effort is made there as in Japan. A joke around Canon Sales Co. is that if we move the operation to the United States, our sales could triple in a few years. The opposite is also true. If we fail in product planning and fumble with introducing a product, sales will plummet about three times faster in America than in Japan.

Despite these differences, I can apply our experience in the United States to sales activities in Japan. We have a big-hit product called Pixel Jet, a Bubble-Jet color copier and printer. It will be a success also in the United States, but we have to know the difference between the two markets. In the United States, an excellent product like this practically sells itself; dealers come to us. But in the Japanese market, we face obstacles. Much is heard about the impediments against foreign products, but they constrict Japanese products, too. In Japan, for some industries, each manufacturer has its own separate dealer network for specific products. Even though we have a big-hit product in the copier industry, it will be sold mainly through Canon dealers. Nonetheless, I am also trying to sell our Pixel Jet through the dealers of other manufacturers. We are getting good response when-ever these rival copier dealers do not have anything like our product.

In short, America is much more open to new sales

channels, while the Japanese market is still very conservative and poses obstacles to changing established distribution channels. My challenge is to create new sales channels
in Japan. Maybe the top management of other Japanese
companies is hesitant about this kind of thinking, but it is a
big insight gained from my U.S. experience. When I went to
the States, Canon did not have any sales channels, so I am
accustomed to trying new outlets. Among other things, I
have set up a chain of Zero-One shops that retail both
American and Canon computers in Japan.

Initially, I had difficulty getting managers for these
shops, but in 1989, I drew upon my American experience.
I called in a key manager and told him that our methods
must change to meet the goal of establishing 100 shops as
quickly as possible. So we had to use the Chicago system.
He was puzzled until I quickly explained, "When I was
serving in America in the 1970s, I was organizing a sales
network. And when opening a Chicago branch, I could not
find enough personnel and appointed only a branch manager. That was Takashi Fujimura, now managing director of
our company, but then only about 30 years old. Fujimura
left for Chicago alone, stayed alone in a hotel while looking
for an office, employed staff, found his own apartment,
increased dealers, and somehow gave shape to our office in
a year or so. Soon after, the Chicago branch grew rapidly."

Within a few days, we adopted the system in Japan to
speed the opening of our computer shops—opening eight
within a year. The only difference was that our Japanese
staff gave the technique a different name, the parachute
shop-manager system. Nonetheless, the Chicago system
(by another name) has worked wonders for our sales in
Japan.

18

My Adventures Selling Apple Computers in Japan

One autumn day in 1983, Masaya Fukushima, the first president of Apple Computer Japan Inc., dashed into my office with an introduction from Bank of Tokyo. Apple Computer had decided to push into the Japanese market—and he proposed making my company its exclusive sales agent.

After listening to his ideas for about half an hour, I immediately said, "All right. We'll have to work out the details, of course, but let's do it."

He looked at me in blank amazement for a moment. He had researched 23 potential partners and intuitively knew that my company was the right one. Still, Fukushima must have wondered whether I was out of my mind. Ordinarily, no president of a listed Japanese company would give a ready answer to such a proposal without much examination and discussion. I learned later, in fact, that he came prepared to give me a sales pitch that would have lasted three to four hours. Apple's proposal, however, was like a gift from heaven because it came at just the right moment.

Fukushima seemed to me almost an angelic messenger. I was just considering how to build up independent businesses so that Canon Sales Company could be listed on the Tokyo Stock Exchange. His proposal fit in perfectly with my plans to start three new activities—sales of imported products, software, and a retail chain called Zero-One shops for office equipment. Becoming Apple's exclusive distributor in Japan was just the sort of import business for which I was searching. Apple would serve as an eye-catcher in our new shops, making them distinctive from others in Japan.

Once I explained all that to the startled Fukushima, he finally understood the reason of my quick answer, and we signed a three-year contract. Our relationship with Apple, however, did not go smoothly at the start.

I can never forget my first meeting with Steven Jobs

and John Sculley in 1983 at the Apple Computer headquarters in Cupertino, California. Jobs was still an attractive young chairman of 27, always wearing a light-blue shirt and jeans. He was really a man of genius and never changed his style or attire—even when meeting a company president like me. John Sculley, then president of Apple, struck me as being like a composed British gentleman, but also was wearing a light-blue shirt and jeans like Jobs.

Their way of life impressed me as reflecting the strength and brightness of the American frontier spirit. Every country has its special merits. And there are many things we Japanese must learn from outstanding Americans who value originality and exert themselves to create something new.

Nonetheless, my encounters with the top executives of Apple also were heated at times. The lack of Japanese software hampered our sales. Not until nearly the end of our three-year contract could we introduce a Japanese-language version of the Macintosh and find other Japanese software for it. Looking back now, it was a natural path everyone has to follow in developing something new, but those were frustrating days. Frankly, Apple Computer and my company did not fully understand each other when we signed our first contract in 1983.

In my initial talks with Jobs, I explained that establishing Apple Computer in the Japanese market would require both time and investment to set up dealers and train our salespeople. It would be impossible to cover those big up-front expenses unless Apple sold us its computers for 40 percent of the suggested retail price. In other words, we needed a 60 percent discount.

Jobs grew angry and asked, "Well then, how many units do you think you can sell monthly in Japan next year [1984]?"

I replied: "Around 100 to 200 units per month until we can introduce the Japanese version."

He then asked, "How many personal computers over 16 bits are sold in Japan annually?"

"About 1 million or so."

Jobs said: "Then even with a market share of 10 percent, Apple should sell 100,000 units a year. You say that's impossible because there is no Japanese version, but 100 or 200 units a month is out of the question. If that is the situation, we can at the most give to your company the same best wholesale price offered to American dealers."

"Mr. Jobs, you ought to know NEC's personal computer has an overwhelming market share in Japan and a massive amount of software. It is meaningless to argue about market share when you only have an English-language version of Apple computers. Even after introducing a Japanese version, you should expect we'll have to continue investing until there is more software available in Japanese. It will be impossible for us to compete with Japanese products at the same price offered to American dealers."

From this point on, our talk went around in circles, with both of us gradually raising our voices higher and higher. Fukushima got between us, repeatedly explaining the situation of the Japanese personal computer industry. For all his brilliance, Jobs could not grasp that we would have to invest heavily for two or three years in building sales channels in Japan; only later would we see any profits. But mutual understanding was not easily reached, especially since the English-language version of the Apple computer had started to make a good showing in the European market.

Finally, Sculley took on the role of peacemaker and

settled upon a price that was a compromise between what I wanted and what Jobs was originally willing to give. I promised that we would sell at least $100 million worth of Apple computers within three years.

At the end of 1986 when our three-year contract with Apple Computer was about to expire, Apple advised us that we would no longer be its sole distributor in Japan. The American company's representative explained that only in Japan did Apple have an exclusive sales arrangement and its global strategy called for using multiple sales channels. We would still be an important sales agent, Apple assured us.

I responded rather unhappily, "Now, when at last Macintosh has started to sell well in Japan, I think it is unfair to make us non-exclusive. We have gained no profit so far, but only made investments. It is about time to recover our investments. Just when the foundation has been built, it is selfish of Apple to create competitors for us in Japan."

The Apple executive reminded me that, as president of Canon U.S.A., I had done precisely the same thing with our exclusive sales arrangements in America. He added, "So you should understand our position."

His words went right to where I lived. It was true that I had obtained an unconditional release from Bell & Howell, which had been our sole agency for cameras in the United States for over 12 years. Then I succeeded in canceling our calculator contract with Monroe and our copier contract with Saxon in America. Fortunately, that has led Canon's U.S. company to attain sales of over $4 billion a year.

As a saying goes, "Samurai must understand each other." The American samurai at Apple must have studied well. He touched my most vulnerable point, so I had to show the magnanimity of a true samurai. At a meeting with Chairman Sculley of Apple in 1991, he really soft-soaped me, saying that our company is the greatest agent in the world. Maybe it is true. We still sell about half of the Apple computers purveyed in Japan, a volume of around $500 million annually.

The personal links that started with Apple have continued in surprisingly different ways. Steven Jobs left Apple to set up NeXT Computer Inc.—in which Canon Inc. is an investor. My company has distributed his computers in Japan. In early 1993, Jobs decided that NeXT would concentrate on selling its unique software, rather than computers, but Canon Inc. remains an investor. Fukushima, who served as my patient go-between with Apple, finally left that company in 1985 and spent six years at another U.S. firm. Maybe an invisible string ties us together, for he is now our chief of software research and development. Business activities constantly change, but personal relations are often more permanent, at least in Japan.

19

The Quasi-Socialism of Japanese Corporations

*W*estern businesspeople who want to succeed in Japan must understand that our companies operate in a style that is partly socialistic. It is not, of course, the ideology that left-wing politicians like to talk about, but maybe our corporate attitude is a kind of socialism.

American top managers pursue profits for themselves and their companies. But what I say in management meetings is more like what one would expect to hear in labor union meetings. In Japan, a president like me thinks in this way: Legally speaking, the company is owned by stockholders; yet the employees and I also feel that the company is ours. So at the stockholders' meeting, naturally I speak in harmony with the commercial laws. But every day we run the company as if it were ours. This makes a big difference.

Because the company is ours, we try to accumulate big profits as internal financial reserves. Consequently, foreign stockholders complain that even highly profitable Japanese companies still keep their dividends comparatively small. Certainly, compared to outstanding companies in Western nations, corporations that are regarded as excellent in Japan tend to have a lower rate of distribution of dividends. But Japanese executives don't get high compensation either. Our corporate life is still conditioned by the disastrous ending of World War II for Japan, which flattened everybody to equal terms.

Chief executives of many big American corporations have been criticized lately for getting huge compensation— up to 10 times what top managers get in Japan. The Japanese people frown upon the idea of senior executives commanding huge pay—and Japanese executives rarely complain about their compensation. They have a kind of egalitarian orientation that was born from the severe economic environment just after World War II. Most of today's

169

top managers grew up before the war, which ended when I was 15 years old. We all shared the common experience of working hard to rebuild the country.

At our national managers' meeting last summer, I purposely said that "we" workers must earn our bonuses. Everyone there understood this; no one thought it was strange. Normally, that is the kind of speech you would expect to hear from the head of a labor union, not a chief executive. Nonetheless, the attitude that it reflects is not peculiar to Canon, but is common for all our public companies. In Japan, the company president and all employees are in the same boat.

Once foreign businesspeople understand Japanese-style corporate socialism, our system does not seem to be such a big obstacle. IBM Japan, for example, has truly melded into the Japanese business environment; it is a U.S. subsidiary but operates like a Japanese company.

I believe that some aspects of our corporate life will change gradually. Immediately after the war, relatively few people invested in company shares. Now, however, more and more Japanese are counting on the income derived from investments for their retirement. Therefore, corporations must begin to consider improving returns to shareholders.

The tax system forces Japanese companies to operate in a socialistic way, but has some negative aspects. One bad practice is the extremely high rate of taxation on property that is inherited. People who inherit a small house or land of, say, one-tenth of an acre in the Tokyo area have to pay half of the value in taxes. That requires Japanese to sell off half of the assets inherited by each generation. This needs to be changed, but nobody knows if it will be.

20

What I Look for in Choosing an International Partner

ost Japanese executives tend to judge Western companies, especially banks, on the basis of their prestige. But I look for something different: good partners with whom we can form really cooperative relationships. That is much more important than so-called prestige.

After my company obtained a listing in the first section of the Tokyo Stock Exchange in June 1983, we planned our first foreign bond issue, denominated in Swiss francs. But we had a problem deciding which Swiss bank would serve as the lead manager. Most board members of Canon Inc., our parent company, recommended one of the three major Swiss banks. Their choice was natural because the big three in Switzerland have the most financial power and the highest prestige.

Nonetheless, I selected the smaller, lesser-known Swiss-Italian Bank. A big reason is that I very much liked its Tokyo representative, Vittorio Volpi, a well-educated person who has lived in Japan for about 20 years and understands the Japanese people well. In 1989, his chairman visited our company, and we proudly mentioned a survey by Nikkei Sangyo Shohi Kenkyujo, a consumer research institute, that appeared in the Japanese newspaper *Nikkei Sangyo Shimbun* and rated Canon Sales Co. as number one in sales vitality among all enterprises in the country. Volpi picked up the paper and translated it aloud at about the same speed as we could read the article in Japanese. I was really surprised by this. He has become an irreplaceable friend.

Giorgio Ghiringhelli, the president of Swiss-Italian Bank, is an accomplished gentleman with degrees from German and American universities, and yet people at Yamaichi Securities in Japan for some reason had nicknamed him "Unsmiling Prince."

After we established our banking relationship, Ghiringhelli would stop by our company whenever he visited Japan. One year, I had an opportunity of inviting both him and Volpi to a traditional Japanese restaurant in Yugawara near Hakone called "Tsubaki," and we enjoyed a meal together. There, the geisha of Yugawara began to sing the old miners song "Tanko-bushi," and we joined in. Soon Ghiringhelli and Volpi, too, chimed in and started to dance by following others. Then suddenly there was a surprise, a change in Ghiringhelli. The "Unsmiling Prince" laughed. I still remember how the people from Yamaichi Securities who were with us that night were deeply impressed to see him sing, dance, laugh, and smile.

After that, we quickly became good friends, and when we issued our fourth Swiss-franc bond in July 1990, we enjoyed a trip to Sicily together on a small jet of Swiss-Italian Bank. Ghiringhelli changed to a jeans outfit, and, with Volpi guiding us, we had a nice cruiser ride off the coast of Sicily. We spent the whole evening drinking, eating, and talking, an unforgettable memory for me.

My other reason for choosing a smaller Swiss bank was perhaps more calculating. If I had picked one of the three major Swiss banks, we would have been just one of their many customers. I figured that we would probably be the most important client of the Swiss-Italian Bank. And that bank did indeed work for us, making the maximum effort to come up with the very best terms. Our bonds carried low interest rates. Besides, our company was in good financial condition, so we did not need the supposed prestige of a big Swiss bank.

Moreover, the bank we selected and our company helped each other. The people at Swiss-Italian Bank never put on airs. They all seem to have a certain gentle quality, probably because they live in such a beautiful city, Lugano. The first time that we issued convertible bonds, Lugano was apparently not qualified under Swiss regulations to serve as the location for the signing ceremony, which was held in Zurich. But as the business of Swiss-Italian Bank expanded, it became possible to hold the signing ceremonies in Lugano. Apparently, our company's bond issues contributed to some extent toward upgrading both the status of the city and the Swiss-Italian Bank. In turn, its low interest rates contributed to the financial stability and power of our company in a big way.

If I had been unduly swayed by prestige, I would have missed a splendid business relationship.

21

How To Maintain Sales Power: A Pep-Talk to Senior Managers

One of the many unusual things that I do is to give every employee a small book entitled *Kigyoka [Entrepreneur] Spirit,* that briefly outlines some of the ideas you have been reading here—my philosophy about business and life in general. This gives people a feeling of belonging to the company, but is far from enough to keep our sales organization operating at its peak. So I have to keep bringing my message up to date, relating my philosophy to the hard realities of the current business environment. Here is an example of how I rally our sales managers:

If there is no youthful enthusiasm and passion for starting new enterprises and trying new methods, then a company becomes filled with tired middle-aged people— and uninteresting. A company that is full of people who understand everything but do little has no appeal; you cannot tell whether its people are alive or dead. That kind of corporation stands in the way of progress, and society is better off without it.

What does a company have to do to ensure that it does not degenerate—and eventually die? It just has to take up new challenges regardless of the difficulties, to have the free spirit of an entrepreneur. Its people should even be a little impulsive, but should not make the same mistake twice. If people did that, the company safe soon would be empty.

We have a slogan "to make marketing interesting," but it is impossible to make things interesting without thinking. Each of us has to become a think tank. We should emulate anything good that others are doing. But everyone—those at the top *and* those at lower levels—has to think and push forth ideas. Wisdom should come from the bottom echelons of the company as well as from the top. And people should never fear differences in views, for the clash of ideas develops into new things.

I have discovered that our younger salespeople do not frequently visit the owners of dealers. Instead, they come to the stores, talk with the staff, and do not show their faces to the owners. It is probably difficult for a 40-year-old salesman to visit a 60-year-old owner. People tend to feel more comfortable with those of roughly the same age group. If you are a salesperson, though, that is a hopelessly inadequate way of behaving. When I became president of Canon Sales, I was about 45 and, looking back, disliked having to meet men in their 60s and 70s all the time. It is not fun at all. But this is a vital part of work, so we must do it.

After getting to know those older men, I had a fairly good time. The same happened to me with golf. When I first returned to Japan, I did not understand why so many people play golf; I used to think there was hardly any connection between sales and golf. At the time, I did not play golf at all. Then I was told that, as company president, I had to hit the opening ball in a tournament. This made me think that being president was a terrible job. Though I am not a good golfer yet, I have been hitting the opening ball for 10 years now. I no longer detest it.

Likewise, you must find ways to develop common topics of conversation with the owners of dealerships—perhaps by talking about golf. Keep meeting the owners, develop friendships, even if it takes years. Then you will have a priceless asset for sales, a relationship of trust.

Never forget our fundamental strategies. First, strive for innovation in building up our capabilities for integration of image and information systems. Second, constantly improve our responsiveness to the diverse needs of customers. Third, foster internationalism by aggressively promoting imports. All these strategies can best be accomplished

by creating a pleasant work environment and showing ap-
preciation to employees and their families through our program for encouraging people to take vacations. And we
must always promote open communications throughout the
company. Only in that way can we all benefit from the
expertise and experiences of every employee.

22

Why You Need to Set Aside Time for Quiet Contemplation

Touring China with a Japanese study group in 1979, I gained invaluable wisdom—about myself. One day, our delegation leader, President Masatoshi Iwamoto of Bunka Broadcasting Co., told me, "Mr. Takikawa, looking at you, I feel a certain menacing quality. You must really be busy, but if you keep on like that, your body will become all stretched out, and it will crack somewhere."

Then he handed me a piece of tissue paper with a sentence from I-Ching (the Chinese Book of Changes): "The measuring worm shrinks so as to be able to gain faith." This means that a worm draws itself together when it wants to stretch out and move forward; in order to grow really large, a person has to bend and yield to accumulate strength. In the ancient Chinese language, it appears that the characters for faith and expansion had the same meaning.

Learning all this was like a sharp smack on my behind. I was so deeply involved in building my company that, no matter where I was, my mind was on work. Without being aware of it, I easily could have been exuding a menacing appearance.

Later, in Japan, Iwamoto, a fine and sensitive person, started to apologize, saying, "Mr. Takikawa, during the trip, I said some things that were presumptuous, and I am really sorry. I am truly embarrassed about that little piece of tissue paper, and so would you please return it to me?"

Instead, I thanked him for his words and explained how much they meant to me. He expressed relief—and presented me with another copy of the same sentence written on fine Japanese calligraphy paper. It is displayed in my office as an important reminder. I have recounted this episode repeatedly to our managers and distributed copies of that saying to them. At one of the companies that we acquired, I used that saying to make a business point: "For the sake of future prosperity, please cut all fat and shrink support departments, just like the measuring worm first shrinks and bends before expanding."

Being given that thought in China probably saved me. Ever since then, I make the effort to create a little time here and there when I make myself think about nothing. While I cannot engage in formal Zen-style meditation, I try to set aside an entire day once or twice a month when I do not meet anyone, I do not open my mouth; I just look at a mountain or the sea.

My calling may be described as "an entrepreneur within a large business group." Pursuing my mission wholeheartedly has caused me to believe that as long as I walk on this path set by Heaven's will, I will be able to accomplish whatever I really wish deeply within.

Unless we wish, feel, and vow deeply about something, nothing will come of it. At the same time, if that something is not in accord with the laws of Heaven, then the more we wish deeply, the more we just torment ourselves. And nothing will come out of it either. My practice of setting aside a day for solitude was partly aimed at going back to nature—and, in my own way, reflecting upon where might be the laws of Heaven.

Much of our worldly desires and inner torment seems to come from the practice of comparing ourselves with others. As I put it, "As long as one does not always compare himself with others, one can be as tranquil as Buddha." If colleagues who joined the company in the same year become section managers, but just one is left behind, that one feels hopeless. On the other hand, if only one becomes a section manager, that one may be full of pride, all puffed up with conceit. If a superrich or famous person favored by the mundane society lives next door, comparing oneself with him will only lead to torment. In such a situation, one cannot get a sense of what the laws or intent of Heaven may be.

Without understanding that, nothing can be realized, no matter how hard one thinks or wishes for something.

Since I am not a Zen priest, I do not sit in meditation, but, instead, concentrate and meditate on the breadth and future of my calling of entrepreneurship, exploring for seeds of new business activity.

Once a mind gets all involved in thinking about something, it is interesting to see how worldly desires and mental torments begin to disappear, one after another. Probably no human being is completely without worldly desires and torments, but they do not occur often when one is using the rational part of the brain. Besides, sticking to the path of an entrepreneur makes life interesting and full of endless possibilities for creating new things.

About 750 years ago, in his book *Shobogenzo*, a Zen priest named Dogen wrote, "Unless you concentrate on one thing, you will never realize an idea." As he put it:

> Nothing can be gained by extensive study and wide reading. Give them up immediately. Just focus your mind on one thing, absorb the old examples, study the actions of former Zen Masters, and penetrate deeply into a single form of practice. Do not think of yourself as someone's teacher or as someone's predecessor.

As I see it, this means: Even if we try to do many things, it is impossible to do everything. We should try to do one thing with all our effort. Furthermore, pretending to be a master or teacher is the most outrageous thing a person can do.

Dogen was writing about religious meditation; but in this modern, expanding, scientific, economic, and cultural world, it is difficult to discover one thing to which one's life can be devoted. After studying Buddhist theology, I have come to believe that my life as an entrepreneur in the image and information industry is my small universe and my calling from God.

23

An Entrepreneur's Personal Code: Never Run Away, Never Lie, and Be Strong with Figures

*T*hree points of self-discipline have sustained my life as an entrepreneur.

Difficulties and pain accompany whatever is interesting, and every day we encounter things that make us want to run away. So my first point of self-discipline is:

NEVER RUN AWAY

I first began telling myself to "never run away" when I was around 30 years old and serving as chairman of the trade union. There was so much conflict that I dreaded waking up in the morning.

Looking back, it is clear that the trade union movement as it unfolded in the 1950s and early 1960s could not digest the ideas of freedom and democracy that were introduced in the postwar period. Japanese people supposedly embraced the great principle: "Freedom means that you are free to do what you want to do as long as you do not harm others." But they often overlooked the second part of this idea—about not harming others. It was a period when many people tended to be "drunk" with a selfish kind of freedom. At meetings of the union and in the workplace, some people felt that they had to oppose everything—even when that opposition ignored rationality. A union leader who catered to those tendencies would not be able to improve the lives of members.

I resolved not to run away from conflicts with left-wing members, but it took a considerable amount of courage for me to advocate legitimate rights and obligations. From about that time on, I often scolded myself never to run away—because I often found myself wanting to do so.

The only way a person can have any authority as a union leader is to have a proven record as a guy who takes on tough problems, who never runs away no matter how difficult things get.

Later, when I became an entrepreneurial president of Canon U.S.A. and sought to cultivate the North American market, I again discovered the need to build up a commanding reputation. Working with people of all races, with varying religions and customs, I had no other way to build a track record except as "that Japanese president who always does what he says, and never runs away."

Given the limited English fluency of most Japanese, it is difficult to move and inspire Americans—and win their trust—mostly through dialogue, no matter how many years one may spend at it. So around this time, I consciously gave myself a second self-disciplinary warning:

NEVER LIE

I felt strongly that American employees gave me more genuine trust from about 1975 when we began implementing a profit-sharing system that I had promised. It was important to keep my word.

If a person is to never run away and to never end up lying, that person must be good with figures. After all, failing to do adequate research and lacking a firm grasp of the facts can inadvertently lead to telling a lie. That naturally led to my third point of self-discipline:

BE STRONG WITH FIGURES

Unless people prepare themselves well, they may not be able to stick to the principle of never lying. And there are probably some who find this so troublesome that they run away from a problem because they do not want to end up having lied.

Therefore, in order not to run and not to lie, there is no alternative except to draw up a scenario backed with rational quantitative figures. I believe that no idea or plan that cannot be developed as a story will succeed. This is what I really mean by saying, "Be strong with figures."

There are other good things about becoming strong with figures. When I was serving as president of Canon's U.S. company, many of our American employees were very impressed that I could cite sales figures in both dollars and the number of units, product by product, without referring to any memo. This partly offset my shortcomings in English and encouraged them to have a little respect. In Japan, too, company executives who are thoroughly versed in the figures impress serious employees and motivate them to work harder.

My three lashes of self-admonition have helped make my entrepreneurial career easier, though nothing worth doing is ever entirely easy.

Index